I write as one who has been perhaps a fond and foolish devotee, and may have done himself little good by it, but I can look back gratefully on many agreeable hours spent—or even wasted in playing. I think not only of quiet corners of many courses, but of many fields where the grass was so long that almost every stroke required a search; I think of a mountaintop in Wales and a plain in Macedonia; of innumerable floors on which I have tried to hit table legs; I recall rain and wind and mud and the shadows of evening falling, so that the lights came twinkling out in the houses round the links, and the ball's destiny was a matter of pure conjecture. Remembering all these things, I can say that I may have been an unprofitable practicer of the game, but at any rate I have been a happy one.

– Bernard Darwin

Golf Charms of Charleston

by Joel Zuckerman · Foreword by Pete Dye

CHARMED BY GOLF CHARMS

As I grew up in Charleston, I learned that golf had an early beginning in the city and that the sport of golf was an integral part of life here for many people. Joel Zuckerman has done a remarkable job of portraying the depth, breadth, scope and richness of the golf life here in our wonderful city of which many are not aware. He has done an admirable job of showcasing our many noteworthy courses, both public and private, and profiling a wide range of the most prominent and accomplished golfers in our midst. Over 4 million visitors come to our area every year, and many of them have golf on their minds. And "Golf Charms of Charleston" explains why they do.
-- **Mayor Joseph P. Riley, Jr.**

Even though I no longer live in the Lowcountry on a full-time basis, I will always consider myself a Charlestonian. Golf has been a big part of my hometown for as long as I can remember, and Joel Zuckerman has done an excellent job of capturing the continuing growth of the game in the Charleston area. Reading this book brings back some fond memories of the wonderful courses and people that have been so important to me throughout my life. "Golf Charms of Charleston" charmed me, as it will you.
– **Beth Daniel - Charleston native and LPGA Hall of Famer**

The grand history of Charleston has been recounted by many authors in any number of wonderful tomes. Joel Zuckerman has added to the lore with his "Golf Charms of Charleston." Lovers of golf will find the book a treasure trove of information and insight. Nongolfers will be given a uniquely different perspective of Charleston. All readers will be enthralled by Joel's energetic and humorous writing style.
– **Roger Warren - President of the PGA of America**

Joel Zuckerman is the Francis Marion of Charleston-area golf. He knows every backwater byway, every key person in the industry, and he is equally adept writing about the low-key, Lowcountry places to play as well as the upscale, four-star venues.
– **Brad Klein - author of "Discovering Donald Ross"**

Astute, entertaining and funny, Joel Zuckerman's new book contains the best essays I've ever read on golf in and around Charleston. If he could putt as well as he writes, he'd be on the Tour.
– **Curt Sampson - author of "Hogan"**

The expressiveness evident in Zuckerman's prose about Charleston makes it clear why he came to visit the area and kept coming back time and again. He certainly wasn't the first to discover Charleston's charms, but is the first to truly reveal them in this very personal, golf-oriented manner.
– **Michael Patrick Shiels - author of "Good Bounces and Bad Lies"**

Joel Zuckerman is wild for golf and he'll go anywhere for a good story. Vagabond Golfer? How about Vagabond Wildman? Zuckerman relays his far-flung golf tales in crisp, entertaining prose that you could hang on the wall like a hunting trophy. Enjoy the book - but stay out of the way of his long irons.
– **Jeff Wallach - author of "Beyond the Fairway"**

Joel Zuckerman displays a great passion for golf, and he places the game (and our obsessions with it) in life's larger context. He goes well beyond the nuances of course design to focus on the people and places in glorious Charleston, the city where the game first came to this nation, and is revered to this day. His attention to all facets of golf brings the game to life on the page.
– **Chris Santella - author of "Fifty Places to Play Golf Before You Die"**

Golfers often talk about "must-play" golf courses. Rarely, however, does the subject of "must-read" golf books come up. Until now. Joel Zuckerman's fine new book on Charleston's vibrant golf scene is sure to find its way into the discourse of serious players in the Southeast and beyond.
– **Ken Baron,** *Golf Connoisseur Magazine*

From the introduction to the index, Zuckerman brings to life Charleston golf in all its colorful and often comical glory. Combining wit and insight, the well-traveled author gives readers a true taste of the city's multifaceted golf scene. You'll want to hit the links by the end of chapter one.
- Peter Rerig, *Charleston Magazine*

Joel Zuckerman covers his subject better and more completely than a high tide. I'd be sure to pack a copy of "Golf Charms of Charleston" before heading on a golf trip to the Carolina Lowcountry.
- John Garrity, *Sports Illustrated*

If you are among the countless millions who haven't played golf with the author - the majority by choice, I suspect - all that you've missed is four hours of laughing harder than you swing, followed by as many hours or more of being regaled with story after tale after barb, ranging from his star (crossed) turn on "Jeopardy" to his daughter's ski-in, ski-out Bat Mitzvah. But you'll get a vivid sense in these pages of what it's like to play a round with the Vagabond Golfer. You'll find the mercurial humor, but you'll also find a keen sense of observation, a sincere affection for the game and a genuine love and respect for life itself. Unlike most raconteurs, Joel writes a story as well as he tells it, and I found myself looking forward to the next chapter in this book as much as I do our next game of golf. If he played as well as he writes, not so much. At least I, like millions of others, can beat him at something.
- Hal Quinn, *SCOREGolf Magazine*

Joel Zuckerman's entertaining journey through Charleston and the Carolina Lowcountry brings to life all the beauty, legends and glories of golf in that golden paradise.
- Dave Kindred, *Golf Digest*

Joel Zuckerman gets after the nuts and bolts of golf as well as anyone, in a way that is funny, honest and sort of hard-boiled. His golf buddies become vivid literary characters, the beautifully described courses of Charleston become stages for the dramas of the game, both large and small, while the sport itself twists through these stories as a fluid, ever-changing and ultimately delightful plotline. Witty, incisive and nicely detailed, these course reviews, people profiles and essays are fueled by the certainty that golf is at once active and meditative, challenging and comforting, and most of all, funny and capable of revealing truths.
- Tom Chiarella, *Esquire Magazine*

Reading Joel Zuckerman's prose is like listening to an old friend weave tales. His opinions - and he has no shortage of those - are clear, and he stands behind them with facts. His grasp of golf and golf history will enlighten those new to the game, while also making this book a pleasure to read for avid enthusiasts.
- George Fuller, *Golf Living Magazine*

Joel Zuckerman, a vagabond golfer if there ever was one, has done it again with his new book, "Golf Charms of Charleston." His extensive knowledge of the Carolina Lowcountry comes through as vividly as the color photos throughout the book. Whether it be public courses, resorts or exclusively private tracks, Zuckerman brings them to your coffee table. His descriptive writing throughout makes you feel, even if you're mired in the dead of Northern winter, like you're on a warm South Carolina fairway. Put your feet up and enjoy.
- Jeff Barr, *Golfweek Magazine*

Letting the rollicking Mr. Zuckerman loose on the grounds of the genteel golf plantations in and about Charleston produces a frisson not unlike his golf swing: abrupt, surprising, unorthodox, amazingly effective, utterly compelling, and vastly entertaining.
– Tom Bedell, American Airlines' *Celebrated Living Magazine*

Published by Saron Press, Ltd.
Design by Michael Reinsch Design
Printed by Regal Printing, Hong Kong, China

Cover art: Courtesy of Charleston Golf, Inc., a non-profit organization supported by the Charleston Area Convention & Visitors Bureau, Charleston Golf Course Owners Association and Greater Charleston Hotel & Motel Association. Pictured is an artist's conception of the first golf course, Harleston Green, and first golf club, the South Carolina Golf Club, in America. Both were established in 1786.

First Edition

Library of Congress Control Number: 2005930695
ISBN: 0-9650791-7-1

Also by Joel Zuckerman:

"Golf in the Lowcountry—An Extraordinary Journey Through Hilton Head Island & Savannah."

TABLE OF CONTENTS

To my mother, whose position at the head of the fan club is unassailable. And to my wife and daughters, the three best reasons this travel writer and vagabond golfer is usually found safe at home.

INTRODUCTION

My writing career began late, and has been propelled by an urgency that might've been missing had I discovered the profession earlier on. It's been a great good fortune that this exigency I've felt to produce has resulted in bylines in some 80 publications in the last half dozen years. Dozens of these have come in journals that are regional, obscure, or even regionally obscure, although there have been occasional sightings in many of the mainstream golf titles. But the flames of this book were fanned by a magazine in which my byline has yet to appear.

Several years ago, the venerable Golf Digest celebrated its 50th anniversary by producing a series of Top 50 lists in a number of different issues. In the "50 Greatest International Golf Destinations," I was struck by Charleston's relatively low rank of 34th. Myrtle Beach checked in at No. 9, and my stomping ground on Hilton Head Island was a single spot lower at No. 10.

There were several off-the-beaten-path golf locales on the list between South Carolina's best-known destinations and Charleston, including curious choices like Whistler, British Columbia; Williamsburg, Virginia; Cape Breton, Nova Scotia; Prince Edward Island, Canada; and central Oregon, among others.

I wondered why Charleston, situated about halfway between the famed golf capitals of Myrtle and Hilton Head, was so overshadowed. Much has to do with the embarrassment of riches the city has to offer. The history, architecture, elegance, nightlife, culture, restaurants and romance of this wonderfully genteel city has much to do with golf being something of an afterthought. Then I realized that - although we had visited Charleston numerous times from our home in Savannah just a couple of hours south - rarely had I thought to bring my golf bag.

Wanting to uncover the mystery of its lowly ranking, looking to raise the level of golf awareness more on a par with the golf behemoths to the north and south, I decided to focus on the fairways of this fine and delightful city. It was hard labor, if you call playing golf repeatedly at two dozen eminently worthwhile tracks and mingling with many of the area's celebrated and accomplished golf citizenry a tough assignment. I packed my sticks, hit the bricks and became imbued in the many golf charms of Charleston. Now you can too.

I had never really spent any significant time in Charleston until 1989, when I was asked to build the Ocean Course on nearby Kiawah Island. Of course, there was no time for much of anything, let alone sight-seeing, when we first went there. After we started construction of a championship course on the easternmost point of Kiawah, it was decided to move the upcoming Ryder Cup Matches from another of my designs, PGA West in La Quinta, California, to the course we were slated to build. The powers that be wanted an East Coast venue so the matches could be shown on live television in Europe. Just as we were getting underway, we got hammered by Hugo, the massive hurricane that blitzed Charleston, Kiawah and the entire area.

All of our heavy equipment was on-site when the hurricane hit. We rebuilt the sand dunes with bulldozers and cleared out the remains of the downed trees and other debris from the marshes so they could thrive again. We generally worked like hell to create a championship venue from scratch that would test the finest players in the world. Most folks think we were successful, and the Ocean Course has been challenging resort guests and professionals alike since it debuted in 1991.

It's very rare to find an East Coast course where so many holes have a view of the ocean, so we were pretty sure we'd be creating something memorable. I've done some of my best work in South Carolina. Courses like Harbour Town, Long Cove and the Dye Course at Colleton River Plantation are all excellent. But nothing I've done in South Carolina, for that matter nothing I've done on the East Coast, compares to the majesty and ambience of Kiawah's Ocean Course.

I'm very happy the golf course is considered the crown jewel of Kiawah, because we think that Kiawah Island has been so beautifully conceived and planned. It goes well beyond the golf. The housing, roadways, bike paths, beaches and hotel properties have all been done with plenty of forethought. It's very much like the city of Charleston itself, which has also benefited greatly by fine planning and studious conservation.

Finally, I've learned my way around the town of Charleston a little bit. The city played host to the American Society of Golf Course Architects annual meeting several years ago. Both my wife, Alice, and I have served as their president. I really enjoyed the ocean vistas at Wild Dunes, where I played in a senior event. I think very highly of Yeamans Hall, and especially love the redan green at Country Club of Charleston. It has always been fashionable to talk about Donald Ross, A.W. Tillinghast and Alister MacKenzie as the giants of golf architecture's so-called "Golden Age" but, personally, I've always been partial to Seth Raynor, who designed both of Charleston's finest traditional courses - Yeamans Hall and Country Club of Charleston.

It's a great old city, truly unique, with a charming downtown and a busy port. I admire the way the city fathers have kept the old landmarks and architecturally significant buildings in such fine condition.

I've not had the opportunity to see some of the area's newest golf attractions, places like Bulls Bay, RiverTowne, Briar's Creek, Daniel Island and the rest. My golf knowledge of the area is still incomplete, but the same cannot be said about Joel Zuckerman, who has written this fine book.

Much as he did in "Golf in the Lowcountry - An Extraordinary Journey through Hilton Head Island & Savannah," Joel offers a comprehensive look at the courses and characters that make Charleston such an intriguing, if under-publicized, golf destination. He has played and described courses from around the world in his writing career, and brings keen insight and a uniquely entertaining perspective to the city's many golf attributes.

Here he melds the old courses with the new ones, well-known Charlestonians with those of lower profile, and spices up the text between with an ongoing series of essays about the game that are both illuminating and entertaining. Reading this book inspires me to carve out some time in my always busy schedule and head back to the Carolina coast to experience all of these golf charms of Charleston.

--Pete Dye

ACKNOWLEDGEMENTS

My first acknowledgement goes to someone with no affiliation to Charleston and even less so with the creation of this book. But I want to recognize my magazine partner in Savannah, nonetheless. Scott Lauretti is the heart and brains behind The Skinnie, and takes on the absolute lion's share of responsibility in putting out our biweekly lifestyle magazine. This frees me up to travel the world, or at least head up US 17 every few weeks to Charleston and its environs. Like a classic deadbeat dad, I was there at the magazine's conception and birth. I even named her, but have been absent for long periods of her formative years. He's had a firm hand on the tiller, though, and our success to date is due largely to his continuous attentions. (And thanks to Scott also for inspiring the subject matter in Section II's final essay.)

Speaking of Skinnie people, I offer thanks to copy editor Suzanne Ramsey. Just like she does with each feature in the magazine, she has carefully examined each of the chapters to follow with a discerning eye. Her style suggestions and copyediting acumen have doubtlessly improved the finished product.

I credit Charleston's Reid and Pat Nelson, who provided occasional shelter, food, forethought, food for thought, direction and directions, among other services. Reid, in particular, was generous with his knowledge (and collection) of fine red wine, advanced pool technique and thorough familiarity with the Charleston golf scene. The first was appreciated, the second tolerated and the last essential to the completion of this project.

In the Charleston golf world, Kiawah's the key, and a couple of key people there made life easier for me. Kiawah Resort's Mike Vegis had a perpetually sunny demeanor, the polar opposite of the weather we sometimes golfed in. Ronnie Musselwhite, formerly of Kiawah Development Partners, shepherded me through the hallowed grounds of the Kiawah Island Club, consisting of two of the finest tracks on the Southeast Coast.

A vague inspiration for this book was Susan Pearlstein, a Charleston charmer if ever I met one. Our friendship germinated in the snow country of Utah, not the Lowcountry of coastal Carolina. But despite the alien locale, she's quick-witted, kindhearted, good looking, an exceptional hostess and a beer baroness besides. As a golf writer, what's not to like?

I've also had dealings with dozens of Charleston's golf professionals in the writing of this book, and they've all been just that - professional. But several fellows have gone above and beyond the call of duty time and time again. I thank Dan Lorentz of Stono Ferry, who's a quality guy and quality golfer, and Rich Rankin of Dunes West, a fellow Red Sox-Patriots-Celtics fan. Alan Walker and his Seabrook Island gang know how to roll out the red carpet, as does Mike Ingram at Bray's Island. Greg Keating of Daniel Island, like me, a Massachusetts man, is a string-puller of the first order. Last but not least, "the Yost with the Most," Jeff Yost of the City of Charleston Golf Course.

Shannon Odom of Charleston Golf Inc. has been a key contact since the very beginning. He's been a sounding board, sage and storage expert concurrently, which is a skill set you just don't see every day.

Brenda Turner has once again complemented the text with her thoughtful line-and-ink portraits, and the book is richer because of it.

My publisher, Paul deVere of Saron Press, Ltd., has yet again produced a quality product. I am grateful to him, and as Paul and I both are, to book designer Michael Reinsch, one of the best in the business.

As is photographer nonpareil David Soliday, who rode in like a white knight on horseback as this project roared to completion, providing some excellent imagery where it had been sorely lacking before. You can't spell "Soliday" without "s-o-l-i-d."

Lastly, I thank my wife, Elaine. Busy with our children and maintaining order on the home front, she rarely found time to accompany me on the numerous reconnaissance missions necessary to write this book. She must've found it vastly amusing that I was gamboling about solo for the better part of a year - wining, dining, opining and reclining when not ambling across the magnificent links of the area. There I was, usually all by my lonesome, in one of the world's truly romantic cities. The irony!

Charleston Golf History for Dummies

This book is not supposed to be dusty. It's not supposed to be musty or fusty. It's not intended to be authoritative or scholarly. Its aim is not as a reference work or textbook. It's just one man's assessment of the leading courses and characters of an underrated golf region, with a handful of opinion pieces on the game in general thrown in to spice up the proceedings.

That said, before the text begins in earnest, this is an appropriate juncture to take a brief and matter-of-fact look at the long and rich history of golf in Charleston. This is a city that has been the site of numerous firsts since it was founded in 1670, and the golf scene is no exception.

Golf is just one of the many areas where Charleston lays claim to pioneer status. Some of the city's firsts are well known, like being the site of the first shot fired in the Civil War, the first decisive victory of the American Revolution and the first public library in the nation. But others are more esoteric. Charleston was also home to the first theater building constructed, and the site of the first opera ever performed in the nation. It's the home of the first Baptist church, formal gardens, science museum, weather bureau and prescription drugstore. It's also the home of the first apartment house, department store, submarine deployment and milkman. It's where the first fireproof building was constructed and site of the first cremation, though whether the cremation actually occurred in the fireproof building or the building was constructed after the cremation went awry is a subject for a more dedicated historian than myself.

The South Carolina Golf Club was formed in Charleston in 1786, which is more than a century earlier than most histories of the game in the United States begin. Scottish merchants introduced the game in Charleston. Not surprisingly, considering the most famous golf society in the world, the Royal and Ancient Golf Club of St. Andrews, Scotland, was formed more than 30 years previously in 1754. A merchant named Andrew Johnston is believed to be the first person to bring golf clubs and balls to South Carolina, though there's no evidence he actually played. His estate included "twelve goof sticks and balls" (an appropriate name, come to think of it) when he died in 1764. He had imported the implements from Glasgow five years before his death in 1759.

Golf was played in some rudimentary form in an area of the city known as Harleston's Green, roughly in the neighborhood of Calhoun, Beaufain, Rutledge and Ashley Avenues, from 1786 until 1799. Farther south, the Savannah Golf Club operated in Georgia from 1795. But both coastal clubs disappeared by 1811, and it was more than another half century before records of the game reappeared in North America. Clubs in Canada and New York were organized later in the century (Royal Montreal in 1873 and St. Andrews in 1888, respectively) kicking off a golf boom that continues today.

There are several reasons why golf was long dormant in Charleston after its early introduction. As mentioned earlier, it was a game brought over by merchants from Scotland and England. Prior to the American revolution, wealthy merchants and planters were on relatively equal footing. But those relationships eventually deteriorated because planters were usually patriots, while most merchants were foreign, often British. Merchants tended to create their fortunes and then return home to familiar shores. As the age of commerce declined early in the 19th century, these merchants moved away and took the game with them, and the next generation of foreign merchants never arrived to take their place.

Antebellum South Carolina society tended to embrace aristocratic sports like horse racing, deeming golf to be a game for the bourgeois. Long after the South Carolina Golf Club ceased to exist, the Jockey Club flourished until the outset of the Civil War. Lastly, as houses proliferated and the streets of the city became more crowded, the game became increasingly difficult to play around Harleston's Green.

It wasn't until the very end of the 19th century that a new golf course was constructed. Chicora Park was a nine-hole layout that debuted in 1899 in North Charleston, on a site that was later incorporated into the Charleston Naval Base. Several years later in 1901, some of the members formed the Charleston Country Club, the forerunner of the Country Club of Charleston. The course was located in Belvedere Plantation on the Cooper River side of the Neck. But in 1922, the club hired Seth Raynor to design a course on James Island and moved there when the course opened in 1925. Raynor's design continues to challenge and intrigue golfers today.

Digesting this information in no way makes the reader an expert in Charleston golf history, not by a long shot. For further enlightenment, one might want to consult "The Carolina Lowcountry - Birthplace of American Golf 1776," by Charles Price and George C. Rogers. But now you have enough ammo in your arsenal to be able to speak with a modicum of authority on this subject the next time it might come up at a cocktail party or dinner engagement. Of course, if this is the most interesting topic of conversation at any soiree you might be attending, you might want to think about finding a whole new set of acquaintances. But just like the 50-odd chapters to follow, that's just one writer's opinion.

-- JZ

SECTION I

The Ocean Course

Ocean Course, #18, Par 4

I was determined to begin my golf exploration of Kiawah Island from the crown on down. There would be no "working my way to the top." The rationale was simple. The rarified world of private-club bastions like Yeamans Hall and Country Club of Charleston aside, the city's golf reputation rests squarely on the shoulders of Kiawah. And Kiawah's golf reputation goes no further than the seminal Ocean Course, wild and windswept, this hallowed and harrowing ground lying in wait on the island's easternmost end.

After unveiling his Hilton Head masterwork, Harbour Town Golf Links, in 1969, what critic would've ever entertained the notion that Pete Dye could surpass himself in the state of South Carolina?

But little more than two decades later he did just that, as the Ocean Course debuted in time for the 1991 Ryder Cup, a tournament that will go down as one of the most memorable, gripping and contentious events in the game's long history.

Kiawah's golf reputation goes no further than the seminal Ocean Course, wild and windswept, this hallowed and harrowing ground lying in wait on the island's easternmost end.

The iconoclastic architect unveiled the Ocean Course in time for The War by the Shore, the biennial team competition between the top American

Ocean Course, #3, Par 4

pros and their European counterparts. Dye worked feverishly to ready the facility come hell or high water, and dealt with a fair share of both. When Hurricane Hugo battered the seaside in 1989, flattening the landscape and toppling trees like dominoes, the architect and his accomplices built the land back up with bulldozers. They recreated the dunes and seascape where a stunning routing had just begun to take shape prior to the monster storm. They finished in time, and the freshly unveiled seaside links bedeviled the Ryder Cuppers to the point where PGA Tour star and former British Open Champion Mark Calcavecchia was left crying on the beach at the conclusion of his singles match.

Dye worked feverishly to ready the facility come hell or high water, and dealt with a fair share of both.

Though it's been tweaked, softened and manipulated over the years, its championship pedigree remain intact. The PGA of America has named the Ocean Course host venue of the 2012 PGA Championship, which will mark the first time the state of South Carolina hosts one of the game's four majors. In the meantime, the course still leaves resort guests breathless and often battered by the swirling gusts, mesmerizing views, ubiquitous waste bunkering and the prospect of trouble to virtually all points on the compass A common saying among the staff is "We don't sell golf balls, we rent them." But despite the intimidation factor, the difficulty, the fact that the greens fee is steep and the waste bunkers deep, golfers flock to the Ocean Course. The reason is simple. It's one of the most memorably exhilarating tests of the game one can ever hope to find.

"We don't sell golf balls, we rent them."

"The Ocean Course is an iconic golf experience in the United States," says Kiawah Resort's Director of Golf Roger Warren. "It provides the opportunity for visitors to play a true links course, which in our country in very unusual. The wind, the ocean and the wonderful Pete Dye design add up to an unforgettable golf adventure that every player should have at least once in his lifetime, although it's been our experience that many visitors enjoy the course repeatedly."

"The Ocean Course is truly unique," concurs Warren's predecessor, Tommy Cuthbert, the original director of golf at the resort, with more than 25 years of tenure. "In this country it is pretty much one of a kind, considering you can see the Atlantic from almost every hole on the site. Pete Dye has done lots of work on the course in recent years, putting in new irrigation, re-sculpturing the fairways, redoing the greens and the tee boxes."

One of the first things a player will notice on an initial visit is that the scale of the golf course is massive. It's fairly narrow and always in close proximity to the beach, but stretches almost three miles in length. But the fact is that the dedicated turf on the course is just 55 acres. The vistas, seascape, wetlands, sand and trouble occupy an area six or eight times that size. Brawny as the golf course appears, with generous fairways and oversized greens, it's dwarfed by the majestic natural panorama that envelops it.

Unless your name is stitched into the golf bag and there is a full-time caddie in your employ, the second thing you might notice is that the course is pretty difficult. Okay, brutal. This thought might occur on the opening hole, if the drive is yanked left and a player must descend a staircase into a waste bunker. Bear in mind, staircases are usually reserved for diminutive pot bunkers; but here, where the sand chasm might stretch to 50 yards in length, you need a ladder to safely reach the bottom. Getting out? Try a smooth mid-iron, a flare gun, a winch-and-pulley system, or some combination of the three.

Want further proof? The second is known by some longtime employees as "the hardest par 5 this early in a round in America." This dogleg requires a drive that needs to carry a yawning marsh, but will go through the fairway into more vegetation if too boldly struck. Then the choice is either lay up short or attempt to fly an insidious little creek with the second. This leaves either a long- or short-iron approach to a narrow, funneling green. And so on. And so on.

"The wind will ratchet up the difficulty factor tremendously," continues Cuthbert. "On a calm day it's very playable, but when it blows it becomes very tough. Sometimes I wonder if people just like to get beat up, because the tee sheet is usually full, and people walk off the course with a smile. They love the scenery, which is spectacular. And the course is certainly enhanced by the legacy of the Ryder Cup, World Cup and Warburg Cup events it has played host to in the past."

Only a real golf hero like the tournament participants Cuthbert refers to should play heroically on the Ocean Course. Anyone of middling ability should

stick with pitty-pat golf, trying to keep the ball on the playing field proper, accepting the prospect of bogey happily, and avoiding the unending acreage of wetlands, marsh, sand and water that surround the playing corridors. Pounding fairway woods into the breeze trying to hit distant greens, cutting corners with the driver to shorten approaches or attempting to land delicate flop shots over bunkers is asking for serious, scorecard-ruining trouble. A fine example of such comes on the 10th hole, a risk/reward par 4 of either 440 or 380 yards from the gold or blue markers, respectively. If the tee shot flies over the cavernous fairway bunker on the right side of the fairway, the downslope beyond will shorten the approach considerably. But coming up short is an ugly scenario. Ruing that they didn't play safely to the left of the hazard, a player standing in this sandy abyss will be looking up at a 10- or 12-foot lip. Forget about seeing the flag. You won't even be able to see the fairway.

For all the trepidation and travails awaiting, the Ocean Course is a special experience. For those who love the game in its natural state, it's a walking paradise with a fine caddie program.

For all the trepidation and travails awaiting, the Ocean Course is a special experience. For those who love the game in its natural state, it's a walking paradise with a fine caddie program. Some sort of permitting glitch as the course was hurriedly being readied for the Ryder Cup resulted in the clubhouse being located a good stretch from both the first and 10th tees, and the ninth and 18th greens. Fortunately, a dependable shuttle system whisks walkers to and from these starting and ending points seamlessly. Once on course, the walk between greens and tees couldn't be easier or more natural. The "cart path only" directive issued by Roger Warren near the beginning of his tenure was a masterstroke. Not only is this a golf course that's meant to be walked, but turf conditions have improved dramatically since the buggies were banished to the periphery.

It's easy to look at the Ocean Course in all its grandeur as predominantly a challenge from tee to green. But the green complexes have incredible variety. Look no further than the twisting, turning par-5 11th hole. This is a crazy quilt of waste areas, wetlands, pot bunkers and grass depressions where the elusive target is an elevated green often buffeted by wind. While a player is aware of the ocean at a distance when playing the front nine, one can't really feel it. The inward nine offers the intimate views of the Atlantic. The dramatic plateau green on the one-shot 14th hole is the closest intersection of surf and turf on the course.

The Ocean Course is slightly reminiscent of what is generally considered the world's finest golf course, Pine Valley. Just like the legendary track in southern New Jersey, there is room throughout the course, and the unending series of carries aren't overly daunting. But just like at Pine Valley, miss it in the wrong spot on the Ocean Course and there'll be hell to pay, it'll be hell to play, and you'll play like hell. Probably all three.

From the blue markers at 6,750, most any golf mortal will have all they can handle. That's why there are plenty of options and numerous tee boxes that will allow shorter hitters and less-skilled players the opportunity to enjoy this incredible track. But be sure to face away from the fairway every so often, and with your caddie's assistance, take a gander at some of the back tees. Never mind that the tips play 7,350

yards, that's a relative pitch and putt. The hard-to-fathom fact is that the course can stretch all the way out to 7,900 yards, if necessary, with a 155 slope and a 79.8 course rating. If the wind blows at 30 m.p.h., as it easily can, nobody, not Tiger, Vijay, Ernie or Phil could break 80 unless they were having an exceptionally fine day. Now that is a tough golf course!

At the Ocean Course, you don't play into the teeth of the wind. You play into fangs.

Remember that there is generally no prevailing wind direction. It can come from anywhere and everywhere. At the Ocean Course, you don't play into the teeth of the wind. You play into fangs. Just do the best you're able, and try not to lose one of the most thoroughly invigorating psychological and physical battles you'll ever find in this great game.

Ocean Course, #6, Par 4

*M*y hopes of conducting an on-course interview with Kiawah Resort's Director of Golf Roger Warren never came to fruition. It's often said that one of the best ways to get to know someone quickly is to spend time with them on the golf course. But it's not quite fair asking Warren to while away the morning with an interloping writer, answering silly questions while assisting in the search for errant tee shots. On any given day, his desk is awash in paperwork, his schedule tighter than Kirstie Alley's stretch pants. It would be like inviting a panhandler into a Porsche boutique. They say that time is money, and while both men might love the opportunity to indulge, the pauper hasn't the money and Warren hasn't the time.

> *His desk is awash in paperwork, his schedule tighter than Kirstie Alley's stretch pants.*

The most notable facet of Warren's remarkable story is not the dual heights to which he's risen— the director of golf at one of the sport's most prestigious destinations and the president of the PGA of America concurrently. It's more about his late start. Warren spotted the competition some 15 years. He didn't come to the golf industry full-time until age 36, and wasn't even a rank-and-file member of the association he eventually spearheaded until the age of 40. Prior to that, he was an educator and a basketball coach, with some time spent as the high school golf coach. But as he's quick to point out, "I've worked at a golf course or a driving range in some capacity since the age of 12." Pay was presumably irrelevant at the outset, because what adolescent boy wouldn't relish the chance to drive a Farmall tractor to pick the range, particularly a heartland kid from Galesburg, Illinois?

Although he never played competitively, he developed a love for the game during these summer dal-

liances. Golf was on the periphery as he concentrated on track and then soccer, obtaining his undergrad and master's degrees in education through the Illinois state university system. Most teachers supplement their income with summer jobs, and Warren was no exception. He worked for some 15 consecutive seasons at the Village Links of Glen Ellyn, a 27-hole municipal about 30 miles from Chicago. Over time, he progressed in his "regular job" from a high school physical education and health teacher to the chairman of the physical education department and head basketball coach. But when the position of director of golf opened up at his summertime employer in 1986, Warren considered making a bold career change. "I had been a shift supervisor at the golf course, and had worked in virtually every capacity over the years. I had been a cashier, a ranger, a starter and almost every job there was to do, albeit on a part-time basis."

He had never dabbled as a director of golf though, nor had the hoop coach any PGA accreditation. But his interpersonal skills and consummate professionalism captured the day. Warren won the job over seven other PGA professionals. "It was a unique situation," he recalls. "All eight finalists were interviewed concurrently in a group setting by about 30 people. I was offered the job, and decided to change course." He began his new career on April 1, 1986, ironically the exact date he took the reins at Kiawah 17 years later. "I was lucky. I was 36 years old at the time, and though I had worked at the facility on a part-time basis for many years, I was competing against seasoned golf pros. My ability to communicate a vision of how I would improve the facility impressed the decision makers."

His recall of that interview some two decades past sounds remarkably similar to the sentiment that won him the coveted Kiawah position just a few short years ago. "My years as a teacher had honed my communication skills and apparently I was a good interviewee. They took a risk, and gave me the position."

The longtime educator sought education himself, and became immersed in the PGA of America apprentice program as he adapted to his new career. Several years later, at age 40, with several golf seasons under his belt at the busy daily-fee facility and many years of real-world experience prior to that, he was encouraged to run for a board position in the Illinois section of the PGA.

There were two new arenas for Warren to familiarize himself with. While his political career was in the nascent stages, he moved nearby to a brand-new facility called Seven Bridges Golf Club in 1991. He continued to move up the ladder both professionally and politically. He went from head pro to general manager in less than two year's time, and in the 13 total years he spent at Seven Bridges, he ascended through the political hierarchy as well. "I worked my way through all the seats locally," explains Warren, now in his mid 50's. "I had been secretary, vice president and president of the Illinois section. Eventually you can move into national politics as your network expands, as you attend meetings and seminars on a regional or national basis."

With his national profile raised, a mutual friend of the golf pro and Kiawah Resort owner Bill Goodwin recommended Warren for the post that longtime director of golf Tommy Cuthbert was getting ready to vacate. "The exposure I was receiving from my political networks helped me get my foot in the door," admits Warren. "But you don't fool people in our industry. You have a reputation both politically and for what you've accomplished in the business. The job I had done at Seven Bridges and the previous affiliation at Glen Ellyn helped me convince the Kiawah management I was the right person for the job."

According to Prem Devadas, managing director of Kiawah Island Golf Resort when Warren was hired, "We obviously considered a number of people for Roger's position, particularly when we were replacing someone who had been here as long as Tommy Cuthbert. It was certainly an important decision, and truly the first time we ever had to make a decision like this, because Tommy had occupied the position since the beginning."

Devadas describes what might generally be considered Midwestern values when detailing the reasons the Kiawah brass ultimately chose Warren. "His character impressed us. He's very honest, hardworking, determined and quality-oriented. All of those personality features stood out. He clearly understood the mission, which is to elevate the resort to a higher level of quality in the quest to make Kiawah the best golf resort in the country," continues Devadas, who spent a dozen years on the island. "He relished that challenge and was confident he could achieve our goal. Furthermore, from a business standpoint, he really understands the financial component of golf. He has a great desire for Kiawah to become the very best. It's a passion for him, and I found it a joy to work with him."

> "Roger is a very driven person, a very smart person, and would like to be associated with a place that's the best there is," offers Tommy Cuthbert, now the resort's director of instruction.

The man he succeeded in the position concurs with the theories espoused by the former managing director. "Roger is a very driven person, a very smart person, and would like to be associated with a place that's the best there is," offers Tommy Cuthbert, now the resort's director of instruction. "If you think about it, there aren't many places that have the potential to be the very best. Most courses, resorts or destinations are hampered by budgetary concerns, physical assets or geography. Kiawah Resort could literally be the best golf destination in the United States someday, if not the world. In fact, some people think it already is. Roger has so much on the ball, and wants to be part of the very best. He and his family have quickly grown to love Charleston, and it's a tremendous opportunity for him to have a long-term association with a resort that enjoys such world renown."

While running his five-course fiefdom spread out over some 15 miles and being responsible for close to 250 employees during peak season is a daunting task, Warren also pays very close attention to his "hobby." As president of the PGA of America through 2006, Kiawah's key golf staffer represents 28,000 members of golf's largest professional association. "I was vice president of the organization while going through the

Kiawah interview process," he explains. "It was a foregone conclusion I'd be named president. Prem and Mr. Goodwin knew the time commitment my PGA duties would entail, and I outlined for them how I'd be able to handle both jobs." His systematic organizational skills and motivation to raise and burnish Kiawah's reputation won him the job, clearly one of the plum assignments in the golf industry. But is it all too much? Did the April Fools Day inauguration on Kiawah portend the things to come, or was it just a springtime day on the calendar?

"To go from managing one course to five was a large adjustment," he acknowledges. "But it wasn't five times as difficult. The systems and the skills I developed in my previous duties were transferable, and while it hasn't been easy, it's been easier than I thought it was going to be. One thing that has been a very pleasant surprise is how much I've grown to love this place very quickly."

"I'm gone from my duties on Kiawah between 90 and 100 days a year," says the politico. "That leaves me 260 or so days a year to carry out my duties here and not much time for anything else." While his high-profile position adds some prestige to the Kiawah package, Warren is a pragmatist. He realizes a resort guest confronted with bumpy greens or patchy fairways couldn't care less that the director of golf is PGA president. "I'm a bottom-line guy, as are my employers. My ultimate responsibility is to this resort, and making sure that the facility performs to the standard of excellence we're trying to achieve and continues to be profitable."

Warren admits it's a balancing act. He's responsible to two major entities, both of which demand focused attention. "With the PGA of America, we're accountable to our members in many ways. We support them in their jobs and try to help them raise their performance and their lives in the industry. We're also attempting to continue to grow the game, specifically among adults, to insure golf remains healthy and prosperous."

Some of Warren's initiatives include an education program that helps certify pros at certain levels to show an employer (or potential new employer) how proficient a candidate is in a measurable way. "This PGA Certification Program is like the AMA," explains the president. "We can certify performance on a regular basis." Members can test their strengths and weaknesses in different facets of their jobs, and

then take online instruction to bolster their performance in weaker areas. "Play Golf America is a program initiated by the preceding president, M.G. Orender. We want to bring more adults into the game, and get adults who've played previously back into golf. Rounds have diminished in the last several years, and while we've clearly been the leader in terms of junior golf programs over the years, we'll continue to be. But we're concentrating on bringing more adults to the game." Warren smiles and adds, "after all, they're the ones who have the money to play."

Despite the awesome responsibility and raised profile, The PGA of America presidency is a completely volunteer position. Warren volunteers that without the dedication and commitment of the dual staffs both on Kiawah and at the PGA of America headquarters in Florida there would be no way to fulfill his duties effectively. "There are great people in both organizations that assist and support me, and are instrumental in our success. If that weren't the case, I'd be much more stressed."

A typical Kiawah workweek is six days, normally 10 hours each. Sundays are usually spent with his wife, Mary, and 20-something son, Michael. The PGA of America duties require four or five annual trips of a week's duration with assorted one- or two-day trips mixed in. "If I'm gone for a couple of days on PGA business, then I'll just work the weekend to catch back up."

Despite his divided attentions, Kiawah Resort is thriving under Warren's stewardship.

Despite his divided attentions, Kiawah Resort is thriving under Warren's stewardship. His directive to make the signature Ocean Course a cart-path-only facility has encouraged walking, and improved course conditions dramatically. "We are very focused on upgrading our service component, our consistency of conditions, maintaining an enjoyable pace of play. We want to compare favorably to all the great resorts in our country, whether it's Pebble Beach, Bandon Dunes or Pinehurst. We have five varied championship golf courses, an incredible city nearby, and now that we have a world-class hotel like The Sanctuary, there's no reason we have to play second fiddle to anybody. We have all the physical components in place. When we can achieve and then maintain the standard of excellence we're shooting for in terms of service, we'll be at the top of the heap."

The former managing director concurs. "Kiawah is on the way to becoming the greatest golf resort in the nation," cites Prem Devadas, referring to a Golf Digest accolade naming Kiawah's service component as the finest in the industry. "That was an express goal of Roger's when he took over, and he's accomplished it rather quickly. It wasn't by accident. It was through implementation of a new plan based on upgraded standards. This is one indication of Roger's effectiveness. Playing rounds are on the increase. The delivery of the improved product correlates with the recent increase in business. Balance sheet aside, golfers can visibly see the difference and improvements in the quality of the product."

"My experience has been that people already know when they've screwed up or made a mistake," explains the director of golf, theorizing on the management style that has served him so well in his career. "They don't need to be reprimanded as much as they need to be encouraged or congratulated when they've done something right," concludes Warren, who has every intention of culminating his professional career at Kiawah many years from now. "They should be told when they've made a good decision."

And it doesn't take more than a precious hour's time in the presence of this ultra-focused and motivated golf executive to realize that upper management made a very good decision of their own when they pegged Roger Warren to become only the second director of golf in Kiawah Resort history.

Cougar Point

KIAWAH ISLAND RESORT

Cougar Point, #17, Par 4

*I*t's an exaggeration to say that Cougar Point has had more makeovers than Madonna. But the delightful resort course that exists today thankfully has little in common with its various predecessors.

> *"The new Cougar Point is much friendlier than the old course."*

When Gary Player was commissioned to build a course on Kiawah in the mid-70's, the powers-that-be wanted an executive-style track, par 62. During the construction process, cooler heads prevailed and it was decided that the course should be of a more-traditional length. What was then known as Marsh Point was stretched to accommodate 10 more shots on the scorecard, but it's a stretch to call the par 72 that was created a championship test of golf. Multiple cross hazards, severe banking and severely sloping greens were just three of the quirky characteristics of the island's original golf course.

"The new Cougar Point is much friendlier than the old course," says Tommy Cuthbert, who ought to know. He was the first head pro at the former Marsh Point, coming onboard in the spring of 1976, several months before the course ever opened. "The greens are bigger and flatter, there's not nearly as much undulation," continues Kiawah's longtime director of golf, now the director of instruction. "The fairways used to all slope towards the water, while now they

12

are much wider. You can hit the ball and it'll actually stop in the fairway and not run towards the water. With the river views and increased playability, it's become much more popular in recent years."

Ric Ferguson has been working as a golf professional on Kiawah since the late 80's, including a stint as Cougar Point's head pro. He picks up the story. "Tommy is right, this has become one of the most popular courses on the island, but that wasn't always the case. When it was originally built, it was short and a bit gimmicky. Gary Player was thrilled to come back and revamp the course about 20 years after the original construction. There were several million dollars in the budget to work with, and he spared little expense, and succeeded beautifully in making it more playable. From the back tees at almost 6,900 yards, it's got everything you want in terms of challenges. Move up a box or two and the course becomes much more approachable by the less-skilled player."

Cougar Point has as benign a beginning as any course on Kiawah. A straightaway par 4 of less than 350 yards from the blue markers, featuring bunkers well on the periphery of the landing area, and an undefended green. This is in direct contrast to the home hole, another par 4 under 400 yards in length, but with a tough drive between water and woods, and a grip-tightening approach to an angled green perched behind water. Between the trouble-free first and frightening finale are a mostly sweet 16 of wonderful variety. Some holes are short, others are long, there are doglegs both right and left, par 5's where reaching in two is a viable option, and others which require three precision shots. There are forced carries on par-3 holes which need to be airmailed, and others that accept a run-up shot.

The visual highlight of Cougar Point comes early in the round. Long views of the Kiawah River are available on the fourth through sixth, the water coming more into play on each succeeding hole. The fourth is a long par 4 of 430 yards, where you can gaze upon the river with no fear. The next is another par 4 that gets closer still, with an approach shot over a tiny sliver of wetlands next to the tributary. The next is a 170-yard par 3 requiring a tee shot directly over the wetlands bordering the waterway.

Preceding this panoramic trio is probably the best par 5 on the golf course, and perhaps one of the best on the entire island. It's a roundhouse dogleg, banking hard to the left. For those without the firepower

to reach it in two, a careful lay-up shot between water and wetlands will set up a short-iron approach to a sizeable green.

Not nearly as endearing is the awkward 15th. It's a par 5 that truly caters to the long hitter able to carry the water hazard and reach in two blows. Station-to-station players have an extremely tricky lay-up shot to deal with. The ball must find perfect placement between a pair of long-limbed trees that might well swat a golf ball into the water hazard fronting the green. It's a bit of a stymie hole.

Another attraction is the well-placed peripheral mounding defining the parameters of the fairways. These high-shouldered bunkers with flashed faces offer wonderful sightlines from the tee, and will often snare an errant tee ball that might otherwise be headed beyond the OB stakes into someone's backyard.

Cougar Point has great balance, with a natural rhythm and flow. Just don't expect to find your rhythm while walking. Self-propulsion is no easy task here. It's a fine course, but one that winds through housing at virtually every turn. Road crossings are inevitable, as are meandering jaunts through various Kiawah subdivisions sure to grind down the soft spikes on your golf shoes. It's a riding course.

Cougar Point has great balance, with a natural rhythm and flow.

Cougar Point, #3, Par 5

Speaking of housing, there are residences all over Cougar Point but almost all of them are unobtrusive. There's very little of the "look-at-me" sensibility that's found in the very few homes dotting the Ocean Course, for example. There are the occasional show-piece homes, but you have to look hard to find them. The dwellings are low profile and blend into the environment, and in almost every case, dense shrubbery and vegetation separate the playing field from the private properties.

In the final analysis, Cougar Point is just a bit reminiscent of a "must play" on one of South Carolina's favorite resort islands. Like Harbour Town Golf Links on Hilton Head, here one must often find the proper quadrant of the fairway to have any sort of look to the green. Placement and working the ball in both directions is just as important as power, an increasing rarity in the modern game. Gary Player's second effort has resulted in one of the finest courses on Kiawah, which makes it de facto one of the best in greater Charleston.

Oak Point

What's in a name? It all depends. Things can be confusing, or not exactly what they seem. On Boston's North Shore, for example, there are a couple of highly regarded private clubs called Essex County Club and Ipswich Country Club. But modern Ipswich is actually in Essex County, and classic Essex is located in a nearby town with the lyrical name of Manchester-by-the-Sea. It's a bit much to keep straight, though it's helpful to realize that the Donald Ross-designed Essex predates the Robert Trent Jones-designed Ipswich by almost a century.

There's a hint of the same obfuscation with Clyde Johnston's eminently playable Oak Point Golf Club. It's officially part of the Kiawah Resort, but is actually located several miles away on Johns Island, and that geographical detail is perhaps the major reason that Oak Point is the most lightly regarded course of Kiawah's numerous offerings. "Because it's not on Kiawah proper, people don't think it's the same quality as our other courses, and are predisposed to think it's not as good a track," says Tommy Cuthbert, longtime director of golf for the resort, who was succeeded by Roger Warren in 2003. "But it's a much better golf course than most people realize. It's fun to play because there's enough difficulty in it to require good shots, but not so penal that any mistake will get you in trouble. The greens are normally excellent, with lots of motion. The river scenery as each side concludes is wonderful also."

The fact is that Oak Point is actually closer to The Sanctuary and most of the rental condos than the Ocean Course or even Osprey Point.

The fact is that Oak Point is actually closer to The Sanctuary and most of the rental condos than the Ocean Course or even Osprey Point, but the "off-island" image can be a sticking point. It's easier to get to midtown Manhattan from the borough of Queens than it is from Greenwich Village, but the latter is in the thick of things and the former is an outlier. Perception is reality.

Oak Point was among the first solo efforts by Hilton Head-based architect Clyde Johnston, who had left the employ of Willard Byrd just a couple of years prior. "At that early point in my career, much of my work had a Scottish influence," claims Johnston. "I was doing some sod-faced bunkers, a bit of pot bunkering, and like many newly minted architects looking to make a name quickly, I probably made the course a bit more difficult than I needed to." There was much to admire about this 1989 design, built as it was on the grounds of an old indigo-and-cotton plantation. But it was underfunded, after completion conditions rapidly deteriorated, and it was a blessing for all concerned when the Kiawah Resort took over in 1997, making it the fifth course in their stable.

Oak Point was among the first solo efforts by Hilton Head-based architect Clyde Johnston, who had left the employ of Willard Byrd just a couple of years prior.

There have been some alterations made to the design since it became an official part of the Kiawah crew, and more in the offing. The par-4 first was lengthened to a par 5, with Johnston commenting that "it wasn't a bad idea." A brand-new ninth hole was constructed, a petite but dramatic par 3 adjacent to scenic Haulover Creek. "I wish the original developer had afforded me the opportunity to build a hole in the same spot. It's really beautiful," claims the architect of record. Plans are tentatively in place to modify the hole further at some future point by digging around the perimeter and producing a peninsular green.

One of the best holes on the course hasn't been altered a whit. The 14th is only about 340 yards, but a large tree encroaching on the left side of the fairway shrinks the effective landing area considerably. To have an unimpeded short iron to the lagoon-fronted green necessitates a tee shot that comes to rest on the far-right side of the fairway. "That's a fun hole," says Johnston. "The property was covered with trees when we started clearing, but we left that key live oak

Oak Point, #18, Par 4

in place as a strategic element."

Another conversation-piece hole is the last, a risk/reward par 4 that borders both Haulover Creek and the Kiawah River. It's a spectacular view with a curious strategy. A finger of the encroaching salt marsh creeps into the fairway, forcing players to either lay up short or blast over the hazard on this 385-yard finisher. Those who can't stomach the 220-yard carry must bunt it out about 200 yards, and have a commensurately longer approach to a green fronted by another wetland. Here again, there are tentative plans in place to modify the eccentricity. The fill generated from the proposed excavation at the ninth would potentially help fill in the cross hazard, allowing golfers to complete their tour of Oak Point in a more traditional fashion.

Another conversation-piece hole is the last, a risk/reward par 4 that borders both Haulover Creek and the Kiawah River.

Beyond individual-hole discussions, Oak Point offers a mostly wide-open sensibility off the tee, with long views of thick vegetation, freshwater lagoons and creeks. It's removed from Kiawah Island proper, and by the same token offers a feeling of remove not consistently found on any of the other resort offerings save The Ocean Course. However, it seems a tad over-sloped. It's a relatively modest stretch from the tips at 6,700 yards, but with a sky-high course rating and slope of 73.8 and 140. Even the penultimate box seems out of kilter. Just 6,360 yards, but rated at 72.3 and 135. Located amidst a housing development called Hope Plantation, the residences adjacent to the golf course are far more modest than what's seen on Kiawah itself, though that's not saying much. Homes almost anywhere outside of Beverly Hills or Monte Carlo are far more modest than the showpieces dotting Kiawah. Oak Point's housing stock is relatively sparse and well set back, and is little detraction from this solid golf experience.

This discourse began with an abstruse reference to my home state of Massachusetts, and so it shall end in a similar fashion. To fully understand Oak Point's position in the Kiawah scheme, I introduce the obscure Danny Ainge Analogy.

NBA basketball fans doubtless remember Ainge, who spent more than a dozen productive years in the league. His greatest moments came as a member of the mid-80's Boston Celtics, where he was instrumental in helping the storied franchise capture a pair of championships. Ainge was a fine and effective player, but was overshadowed on those great Celtics teams by his running mates, all of whom have made or likely will make their way into the Hall of Fame. Larry Bird, Kevin McHale, Robert Parish and Dennis Johnson are among the elite players in NBA history. Ainge was solid, just like Oak Point. But he suffers by comparison to his four teammates, much as Kiawah's golf outpost on Johns Island suffers just a bit in contrast to the quartet of all-star tracks a few miles farther east.

When Danny Ainge left Boston, he continued to play good basketball for several other teams, cementing his status as a long-term quality player. By the same token, in any other locale Oak Point would be considered a top-notch venue in its own right. But in the pantheon of Kiawah's other world-class courses, it's a medium-range jump shot behind.

When Danny Ainge left Boston, he continued to play good basketball for several other teams, cementing his status as a long-term quality player.

He stepped down as Kiawah Resort's director of golf in 2003 to lighten his schedule a bit and become director of instruction, but it'll be at least another generation before anyone other than Tommy Cuthbert is linked as inexorably to the island's golf scene. Like Lincoln on a five spot or Washington on a quarter, Cuthbert is the enduring face of Kiawah golf.

> *"He is one of the most dear people I've ever had the privilege of being associated with in my life."*

"He is one of the most dear people I've ever had the privilege of being associated with in my life," claims Pat McKinney, president of Kiawah Island Real Estate, who first met Cuthbert in the mid-70's while serving on the hiring committee to find the island's first head golf professional. "I was one of the few people on the management team who was serious about golf, and I took a real interest in who we hired. Even as a young man in his 20's, he exhibited a quiet grace, charm and sincerity that was very endearing. We've been very proud to have had him here all these years. Over the decades we've shared many things together, personally and professionally. My respect for him and the regard in which I hold him has only increased over time."

How can one possibly quantify better than 10,000 days of service into a handful of highlights? It's like asking Ben and Jerry their favorite ice cream flavor. Better yet, querying Benjamin Moore as to his preferred color of paint. But Tommy Cuthbert, always willing to answer a fair question, narrows it down to a final four:

"The Ryder Cup was a peak moment, obviously. It was so dramatic, and so memorable. It was great to be involved with it. Spending time with Jack Nicklaus was also a highlight to me, both when he initially worked on Turtle Point in the early 80's and again when he came back to make changes many years later. He's such an interesting person to be around. Likewise, getting to know both Pete and Alice Dye was a thrill. They are such extraordinary people, with a tremendous love for the game. We were together quite a bit during the construction and subsequent revisions Pete made to the Ocean Course. He's so much fun to be around and brings a tremendous amount of energy to whatever he's involved in. I don't think I've met anyone of his age with so much energy. He has so much insight into the history of golf architecture. Just listening to the Dyes talk about golf is tremendously enjoyable. Lastly, and on a very personal level, I would have to say when my son worked as a stand-in for Matt Damon. Jess was a student at the College of Charleston at the time. I had been giving lessons to Robert Redford, who directed 'The Legend of Bagger Vance,' partially filmed here on Kiawah. He had met Jess, and they hired him to be Damon's stand-in. He was so excited and I was so excited for him. When he worked on the movie, he got to meet all the stars, like Will Smith and Charlize Theron. It was a fun and memorable time for him and our family."

Individual moments might be difficult to choose, but ask Tommy the single best thing about his job and the answer comes quickly and definitively. "Meeting people. Kiawah attracts folks from all over the world, and getting to know such a wide range of individuals from all walks of life and various backgrounds has been a wonderful experience. Working under different ownerships has been instructive as I've observed many different types of management styles."

His competitive golf highlight came some four decades past, when he captured the 1966 South Carolina Open Championship as a high school kid, a decade before he started reporting for duty on Kiawah. Tommy parlayed his "teen sensation" status all the way to Louisiana State University, where fleeting Tour dreams quickly gave way to grim reality. "I hadn't been exposed to large numbers of really good players until I went to college," he explains. "I was happy to play some competitive collegiate golf, but quickly saw there were lots of guys as good or better than I was."

He has a certain insouciance one doesn't usually encounter among professionals.

Tommy is still serious about his golf game, but he has a certain insouciance one doesn't usually encounter among professionals. Consider this: From the middle of the fairway he casually removed the cellophane wrapper from a brand-new 3-iron, much the way you'd unwrap a fresh pack of Juicy Fruit. Needless to say, he'd never struck a ball with this particular club before, but without ceremony he unleashed a high-velocity bullet that darted left of the green, ending up pin high. You get the feeling that if he stuck it four feet from the flagstick his facial expression wouldn't have been any different. Summing up a person in a single word is tricky business, but "smooth" isn't far from the mark. Tommy swings smoothly, walks and talks in the same easy manner. He looks a bit like Fred Couples, give or take 10 years and pounds. (Give the years, take the pounds.) And they don't come much smoother than Freddie.

He looks a bit like Fred Couples, give or take 10 years and pounds.

Every so often, Tommy reveals a bit of the champion player simmering below the placid surface. A few holes after unveiling his new 3-iron, he took a more-trusted club from the bag. He lofted a 50-yard pitch shot out of thick rough, over a bunker. It tracked slowly towards the hole, kissed the stick lightly, and though by all rights should've disappeared underground, came to rest perhaps a foot away. I asked him to describe the shot. Was it open-faced? Were his wrists still? Did he purposely let the sand wedge slide under the ball, or did he pop it out? What do you call it? "Luck," was all he said, with an easy, self-deprecating smile.

There's more than luck at work, though. Asked about the rescue club he chose to confront the 180-yard par 3 into a breeze alternating between howling and humming, he commented, "I need to be rescued." The shot tore through the heavy fabric of the wind, settling 10 feet from the hole. Later on, he hit that easy-as-pie, 80-yard bunker shot to 10 feet as well. There's no flash and dash to his game, he doesn't hammer it a mile. But like solid players tend to do, he makes it around with an efficiency of strokes beyond the ken of handicap players. The final tally was 76 on a gusty afternoon at Osprey Point. No course record, but more than respectable for someone playing a full round only once every couple of weeks. "That's pretty much par for me these days," he offered with a laugh and a shrug.

Tommy became director of instruction in the spring of 2003. "I felt the time was right to reduce some of the responsibilities I've had out here for so long. Being the director of golf at Kiawah, as Roger Warren has learned, is a very time-consuming job. With our boys, Walter and Jess, now grown and married, I was ready to have some more time off." Beverly and Tommy have been married for more than 35 years, and are traveling with greater frequency than his schedule allowed previously. San Francisco, Los Angeles, Wyoming and Alaska are just a few of the destinations they've visited in the recent past, with more adventures in the offing.

Tommy feels fortunate that he was given the opportunity to continue his long association at Kiawah Resort by becoming director of instruction. "I wanted to stay in the golf business, and I love being around people and teaching. It was an excellent way to stay closely involved at a place that has been such an important part of my life." As an instructor, Tommy varies his approach, depending on what the player is trying to accomplish and how much time he's willing to put in. "I'm a feel teacher more than a technique teacher. There are specific things that need to be part of any sound golf swing, and I work with each student individually, depending on age, body type, flexibility and other factors. There's definitely more than one way to teach the game."

His office at Turtle Point was 44 miles from his Summerville home. It was some 35,000 automotive miles a year, a total of more than a million miles behind the wheel in a 30-year career. And while there might be as many memories as miles, not quite the same number of lessons given, or acquaintances that became friends, or underlings that went on to bigger things, or assistants that became head pros themselves, or staff meetings, late nights, highlights and hard times, that second number is pretty darn high itself. It's quite a legacy. "It's been a great place to come to work everyday. We've had tremendous growth and challenges over the years, but the beauty of the island and the great people I've gotten to know along the way have made my career a wonderful experience."

"Sometimes it works and sometimes it doesn't," he says smiling. "Like everything else in golf."

One final note about Tommy. He has this rather odd putting style he's been employing for a number of years, claiming it helps his ongoing struggle with the "yips." He turns his right-handed putter over, putts left-handed, and uses the small "toe" on the back of the instrument instead of the blade. "People who don't know me think I'm messing around and not playing seriously. They can be bewildered and not say a whole lot about it. Sometimes it works and sometimes it doesn't," he says smiling. "Like everything else in golf."

Observing this peculiarity, one might be inclined to call it silly, counterproductive, counterintuitive or even "bassackwards." Tommy simply calls it "going backhanded." Despite this obvious eccentricity, what looks to be a most uncomfortable putting technique, spending time with Tommy Cuthbert couldn't be more comfortable. He's a quality guy, personable, in possession of a hard-to-find inner warmth. He's a class act. And that's no backhanded compliment.

Osprey Point

KIAWAH ISLAND RESORT

It's apparently not in Tom Fazio's genetic makeup to produce an unattractive golf course, and Kiawah's Osprey Point is no exception. It's among the most scenic of the Kiawah courses and probably the most moderate in terms of difficulty. This is a fine design with plenty of pleasing holes, but its chief asset might just be how agreeable to the eye the entire golf course is.

> *"Osprey Point is a classic Tom Fazio golf course," offers Kiawah Resort's Director of Golf Roger Warren.*

"Osprey Point is a classic Tom Fazio golf course," offers Kiawah Resort's Director of Golf Roger Warren. "It provides clear views of where a shot should be hit, and offers numerous risk/reward opportunities. A player can choose the line of play and expect good shots to be rewarded and poor ones penalized. That's what golf design should be, in my opinion."

There are four sizeable lakes and fingers of saltwater marshes set among maritime forests of pine, palmetto, oak and magnolia trees that provide a classic Lowcountry look at Osprey Point. Water in one form or another comes into play on 15 separate holes. Sounds intimidating. But the less-skilled player will be relieved to find that the majority of this trouble is located left of the target line on the most forgiving design in the Kiawah oeuvre. "We put the trouble predominantly on the left," says the compassionate architect. "This was a conscious decision, so as not to create an overly difficult playing experience for the typical resort guest, the medium- or even high-handicap player who generally hits it to the right."

The beauty quotient is evident from the opening blow. Osprey Point commences with an attractive par 4 of 385 yards with lovely Pintail Pond running the entire left side of the hole. The par-4 seventh showcases Fazio's love of the short risk/reward hole. Only 320 yards from the penultimate markers, any drive that doesn't fly the large mound and bunker on the right side of the fairway will leave an approach to a green totally obscured by the hillock. Either attempt to fly the unusual hazard complex and have little more than a pitch shot in, or play safely to the far-left quadrant of the fairway.

The outward journey concludes in rigorous fashion. Nineteen eighty-nine's Hurricane Hugo did a number on the staunch ninth, knocking out hundreds and hundreds of trees that helped separate the fairway from the driving range beyond. Nevertheless, this 440-yard dogleg left over water is still a stunner. Pintail Pond comes into play here once again, and this sizeable body of water fronting the tee and left of the fairway seems large enough to water-ski. This is assuming you are skilled enough on skis to dodge the omnipresent clumps of sweetgrass dotted throughout, which turns bright red in autumn. Bite off as much as you dare on the tee shot, because the farther left you traverse, the closer you'll land to the water, but also to the putting surface. Of course, too far left is exactly where you cannot be. More timid souls will go well right, and have to play this toughie as a dreaded three-shot par 4. "It's certainly a strong hole," says Fazio with typical understatement. "It's similar to the 18th, which is routed in the same direction on another part of the property."

The last at Osprey Point vies with Cougar Point and the Ocean Course for Kiawah's toughest closing hole, a 540-yard par 5 that doglegs around another massive lagoon. A player who has to lay up with his second shot will likely find that his ball has come to rest among a curious series of humps and bumps in the fairway, starting about 130 yards out. The odd stance or lie that might well ensue makes a straightforward short-iron approach shot that much tougher. Looking back from the narrow green, the undulations look like a roiling sea, the same sensibility one encounters for real at the Ocean Course, just a few miles farther to the eastern edge of the island. Between these final challenges on each side are a number of noteworthy holes, including the 11th, which is a challenging par 3 over water. The curiously canted green that slopes dramatically from left to right makes an intimidating hole that much tougher.

Osprey Point, #9, Par 4

The 13th is only 345 yards long, but with a constricted landing area bracketed by a bunker right and a waste bunker left. With another massive greenside bunker in play, this hole has more sand, pound for pound, than most any hole you'll see. Speaking of which, the 160- yard, par-3 15th plays over a curious ribbon of a waste bunker, with water well right and left that will swallow any seriously misdirected shot that gets caught in the oft-swirling winds.

"The course was redone in the late 90's, and the members and resort guests really enjoy it," comments Tommy Cuthbert, Kiawah's longtime director of golf, who vacated the position to become director of instruction in 2003. "It's relatively open, though it appears that there's plenty of water in play and there are a few forced carries. But it's really playable. You can get it around the course without losing a ton of golf balls because the playing corridors are fairly wide. The greens have enough undulation to be fun, but aren't overly severe. And with all the lagoons, the views are really beautiful also."

Osprey Point, #3, Par 3

"I began working at Osprey Point shortly after I completed my work at Wild Dunes," explains Tom Fazio. "As part of a master-planned community, I'm proud of the forethought that was given to the design. It's great that the clubhouse looks out over the first, ninth, 10th and 18th holes, as well as the prac-

tice range, with no visual intrusions. As an architect in an ideal world, I'd have golf only, with no houses nearby." An ironic statement, considering that the Fazio course features more showy homes than any other on Kiawah. Osprey Point is one of the island's most prestigious addresses, and the housing is consistently magnificent. It's one showpiece after the next set well back from these manicured, wide-open fairways, and the course isn't just an attraction for golf fans, but real estate fans as well. Not too many starter homes in this part of the world.

The course isn't just an attraction for golf fans, but real estate fans as well. Not too many starter homes in this part of the world.

It's become more prevalent in recent years, but the architect insists that in the late 80's the course was a leader in committing vast areas of open space for the golf aesthetic exclusively and leaving the real estate component at the periphery. "The developers allowed me the latitude to create the course in this way, and it's a testament to their desire to put golf in the forefront."

"Osprey Point turned out wonderfully," concludes Fazio, who's unofficially titled America's Greatest Living Architect. "It was an outstanding merger between a golf and real estate environment. The two are of equal importance, and have mixed together well." And Osprey Point is right in the mix as one of Kiawah's most beloved courses.

Turtle Point

Turtle Point, #14, Par 3

At the risk of sounding reptilian, I've been somewhat snakebit at Turtle Point.

An initial foray during hurricane season took place in a driving rainstorm, a torrent that would've sent Noah himself scurrying for a slicker and rubber boots. Months later, there was a return visit on the cusp of winter. The encore took place under crystalline skies, a chamber of commerce day that would inspire marketing flacks and public relations types to rush out with photography equipment and gather visual material for future brochures. This assumes their shutters would be clicking through a plateglass window, because the morning in question was so frigid they would've frozen their f-stops off.

I joined some hardy, creaking souls on the range prior to the round; the words "warm-up session" were never meant so literally. These were longtime members who could play most any day of the year, and though there can't be five days out of any 365 when the temperatures would be lower, they were ready to take their licks regardless.

At the risk of sounding reptilian, I've been somewhat snakebit at Turtle Point.

"Other than the Ocean Course, Turtle Point is the toughest track on the island," explained one resilient senior who was home on the range in a ski hat and leather gloves. "Why not play the best when conditions are toughest," he reasoned.

"The bunkers are the most consistent and the greens are faultless," added his scarf-wearing cart mate, nipping wedges nearby.

The starter was bundled to the point of mummification but chimed in, "The ocean holes are what make this golf course tick. That's what our members and the resort guests really love, the three short holes that run along the beach." I had to run along myself and supersede the seniors on the tee in the hopes of completing a two-hour solo inspection.

In the final analysis, all of their comments were very much on the mark. The greens, in particular, are definitely worthy of mention. This strain of Tif Eagle was installed in the late 90's when Jack Nicklaus and company came back for some touchups, and they appear to be the finest putting surfaces in Charleston County, never mind Kiawah itself. When we were foolhardy enough to brave that September deluge, the greens were draining perfectly and rolling true. On this ultra-crisp and dry morning they could only be described as pristine.

This is an early-Nicklaus golf course, a bit more low to the ground in nature, without some of the mounding that became prevalent later in his career. Or as a pundit once remarked, "Turtle Point came about before Jack knew how to drive a bulldozer."

Kiawah's Director of Golf Roger Warren elaborates, "It's a unique Nicklaus design because it's a low-profile course with a classic Lowcountry look, but with classic Nicklaus nuances. It requires a high, fading ball flight for the most part, which was his preferred shot shape. All designers go through phases, and this vintage Nicklaus reflects his experiences playing the game. What I like about this course is that he fit the holes on the land he was given to work with, and didn't move a ton of earth during construction. He fit his vision of the golf course on the land in an unobtrusive way, and it works very well."

> "Turtle Point came about before Jack knew how to drive a bulldozer."

The first 10 holes are mostly standard resort fare, albeit at a difficulty level a notch or two above a typical vacationer's track. The 141 slope rating from the 7,050-yard championship markers and the 136 slope from the 6,600-yard blues are testament to that fact.

A hint of what's to come down the stretch is revealed on the intriguing 11th, though, a 380-yard par 4 with water menacing the tee shot and also fronting the green. The 500-yard 13th is the best par 5 on the course. Long-ball hitters can reach it in two, catapulting an approach over the wetlands bisecting the fairway. Short knockers will have to tread gingerly towards the green to avoid the vegetation.

"Turtle Point happens to be my favorite course on the island," explains Tommy Cuthbert, currently the resort's director of instruction and for many years previously the director of golf. "When the course was redone in the late 90's it became a bit friendlier to the higher- handicap player, and at the same time made it a bit tougher for the lower handicap." Cuthbert alludes to the fact that some cross hazards were eliminated that would snare the shorter hitter, while several bunkers were replaced with grass depressions and waste areas. The chips and bump-and-run shots are easier for the less-skilled player than a traditional bunker shot, while a good player would rather just hit a standard sand shot, and not have to conjure a pitch-and-run or flop shot. "It's my favorite course because it requires quality, precision shots to play well."

> "Turtle Point happens to be my favorite course on the island," explains Tommy Cuthbert.

Cuthbert is spot on as usual. Turtle Point requires more precision than most any other Kiawah offering. There's usually room enough to find the fairway, though some holes constrict. It's the approach shot that causes the anxiety. Out-of-bounds stakes loom ominously close to the cart path on numerous occasions, and a faulty second that either drifts right or hooks hard left might well come to rest on the nether side of the dreaded skinny white stake.

Ronnie Miller has been a Kiawah golf pro for more than 15 years, and closely monitored the Turtle Point renovation. "The collection areas adjacent to some of our greens replaced bunkers and rough, affording different options to advance the ball onto the putting surfaces. Several greens were raised and recontoured, and what were mostly smaller and flatter greens now have more movement and flair." Miller came to Turtle Point in 2000, and acknowledges the course's inherent demands. "It's mostly tight, although long par 4s like the eighth and twelfth have generous fairways that allow a player to really try and bust a drive. Many top players truly feel that this is the most difficult course on Kiawah, as the Ocean Course can be rendered defenseless without wind. Here you need precise drives and approach shots the entire round."

The course routing consists of a pair of opposite loops - a counter-clockwise outward nine, and a clockwise return. The memories are made turning for home, as the 14th through 16th holes are adjacent to Kiawah's marvelous beach. Unfortunately, golfers aren't the only creatures who relish time spent by the sea, and this tiny trio of holes, two medium-length par 3's sandwiching a petite par 4, are almost asphyxiated by the adjacent housing. "I think anytime you have an ocean-side experience that gets a bit hemmed in by housing it reduces the overall nature experience you would have otherwise," acknowledges Warren. "But when you have the opportunity to route golf holes in close proximity to the Atlantic as the designer has done, it still makes for a memorable encounter."

Of the three waterside offerings, the 350-yard 15th (playing 385 from the tips) is the prizewinner. The dune line is left and the beach beyond that. To the right is Millionaire's Row, the oceanfront housing nestled behind out-of-bounds stakes. From mid fairway it looks like the target is an island green, bracketed by thigh-high vegetation. It's a visual deception, because the shrubbery and high grasses are actually well short of the ultimate target. There's room to miss both short and right, though first-timers will be swallowing hard as they prepare to execute what looks like an "all or nothing" swing.

Regardless of vagaries in temperature or precipitation, Turtle Point is a compelling adventure. It's fortunate that most players experience the course in the idyllic weather most often seen on Kiawah, and only seldom have to brave difficult playing conditions. Even on a pleasant, shirtsleeve day, the challenge of Turtle Point demands a golfer's full attention.

Turtle Point, #15, Par 4

Halloween was always my favorite holiday as a boy. Trick-or-treating around the neighborhood, coming home with bags full of candy that night, and opening birthday presents the next day. It was quite a one-two punch for a little kid.

I've never forgotten the delights of Halloween.

I guess I'm something of an adult now, at least according to the birth date on my driver's license, and my thrills come differently. But I've never forgotten the delights of Halloween. To pay homage to the holiday and my favorite pastime concurrently, allow me to present The Dirty Dozen, one man's compilation of the scariest golf shots you can encounter. Some of the following scenarios make walking down a darkened, shadowed street in the company of monsters, ghouls and goblins seem like a day at the beach in comparison:

• The long explosion shot out of sand. Bunker shots are problematic for many of us, but having to fly the ball 10 yards in the air ratchets up the fear factor considerably.

• The three-foot downhill curler. Trickle it and try and die the putt in the hole? Ram it and take out the break? Take a deep breath and relax the white knuckles, because you might have a 20-foot comeback putt afterwards.

Take a deep breath and relax the white knuckles.

• Trying to thread a long iron between the trees from close range. Sure, the easier play is laterally. But if you nail it through that narrow gap with a slight cut, you can reach the green. Be wary, though. A near-scratch player I knew once hit a tree and the ball came back hard and knocked out four teeth.

• The par-3 tee shot over water. Take plenty of stick, because we have a tendency to come off the ball, and fade it 'till splashdown.

• The driver off the deck. It's the classic risk/reward shot, when trying to reach that par 5 (or long par 4) in two. Easy to top it or slam it sideways into oblivion, though.

• The chop shot out of the hay. Rarer in the States, more common in the United Kingdom. It's one thing to find the ball in the deep stuff, another thing entirely to make contact. There's nothing more depressing for a semi-competent player than the old swing-and-miss, a distinct possibility in knee-high rough.

• The 35-foot putt up (or down) a contour. No matter how much experience you have, it's easy to let this longish, breaking putt get away from you.

• The bunker shot over a high wall. Not something we see lots of in this area, though Country Club of Charleston and Cherokee Plantation both have their share of cavernous chasms. Get it up quickly, or slam it into the wall and have it roll back to your feet.

All a drive like this does is put pressure on you to hit a short iron close.

• An approach shot after a massive, center-cut drive. A long-knocker friend of mine once told me memorably after I complimented his 290-yard tee ball: "All a drive like this does is put pressure on you to hit a short iron close." True enough, upon reflection.

• The lob wedge from a tight lie to a closely guarded pin. The club will in fact do the work for you, if you let it. But how often does panic infiltrate the swing? A shot that should go sky-high and land close often turns into a chunk into the bunker, or a screaming meemie that finishes three times farther from the hole than where you started.

• The five-foot putt to win the match. It's effortless to miss from this distance, but it won't stop you from hanging your head in shame afterward.

• The first tee shot of the day, executed in front of a gallery. It matters little if said "gallery" is nothing more than the next foursome waiting to tee off, or a table or two of beer drinkers relaxing on the deck. Fact is, to some nervous types the jitter factor is caused by their very own foursome. It's just something about that first tee, though. We hope to make even incidental contact, than either stride or slink to the ball in the hopes we can complete the remainder of our round in blessed obscurity.

The Sanctuary

KIAWAH ISLAND RESORT

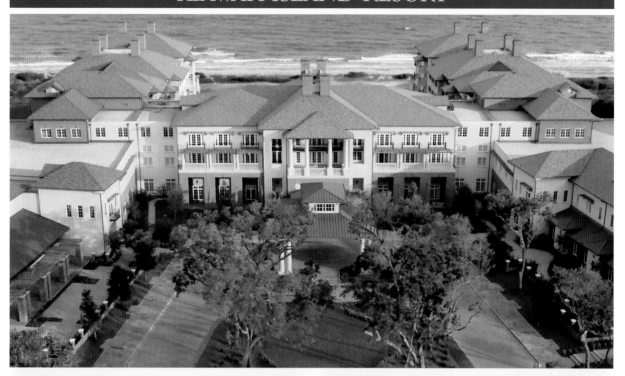

How perfect is the name? According to Webster's Dictionary, a sanctuary, or in this case, The Sanctuary, is "a consecrated place, a place of refuge and protection."

Compare this name to some of the more established grand hotels along the Eastern Seaboard and beyond. A cloister, or The Cloister, is a "state or place of seclusion." Doesn't sound too social, does it? The Homestead is "an ancestral home." The Breakers? The Greenbrier? Heck, The Broadmoor out in Colorado? Just a trio of proper names.

There are untold thousands of words in this book, words about courses, words about characters, sentence after paragraph after chapter. Just this once, we'll let the pictures tell the story by themselves. Take a close look at some wonderful imagery from one of the finest and newest resort hotels in the nation. You'll find no better place of respite between golf rounds.

Crooked Oaks

SEABROOK ISLAND RESORT

Number 18, Par 4

It's not every Charleston-area golf course that can boast of having had Hall of Fame names like Beth Daniel and Nick Price on the payroll, but exceptional Seabrook Island is not just any facility.

...Crooked Oaks is a course where the putter becomes the most important implement in the golf bag.

"I worked in the shop for a period of months between graduating from Furman and attempting to qualify for the LPGA Tour," explains Charleston native Beth Daniel, the two-time U.S. Amateur champion who's won more than 30 events and better

than $8 million in her many years as a Tour pro. She continued working for Seabrook for years thereafter, albeit not in the sweater-folding department. "I represented the island for about seven years when I first got on Tour," recalls Daniel, who's latest claim to fame is being the oldest player in LPGA history to claim a tournament victory. She was well past her 46th birthday when she captured the 2003 Canadian Open.

While Daniel is the real deal, this particular Nick Price is an impostor. He's a 20-something South Carolinian, not a 50ish Zimbabwean. But unlike his multi-Major-winning namesake, this Nick knows the grounds of Seabrook's estimable Crooked Oaks course quite intimately, where he serves as a grounds superintendent. "The greens are the calling card," he

Number 4, Par 4

claims, and borrowing the title of the long-running television game show, "The Price is Right."

Unlike Seabrook's original course, Ocean Winds, a tee-to-green challenge with few equals in greater Charleston, Crooked Oaks is a course where the putter becomes the most important implement in the golf bag.

The greens have recently been converted from Crenshaw bent grass to Champion Bermuda. The changeover was made to the hardier strain to save the expense of potable water, and help alleviate some of the maintenance issues that the more delicate grass requires. It might be a new surface, but the original sensibility remains. Crooked Oaks will always offer quicker, firmer, more dynamic putting surfaces than its older sibling. The most notable facet of this 1981 Robert Trent Jones design is the sizeable greens, which are less accurately described as undulating, and more precisely defined as compartmentalized.

"Unlike our other course, Crooked Oaks is pretty straightforward," explains Director of Golf Alan Walker. "There's no need for guidance from tee to green, nobody needs to tell you where to aim." When the architect created the course, he marched directly through the forests of oak, palmetto and magnolia trees. His philosophy might've been culled from Euclid's well-known postulate that the shortest distance between two points is a straight line.

Missing the greens means descending into cavernous greenside bunkers more often than not, as there is an average of almost two per hole.

Here the fairways are wider, the water more of an incidental presence, the ball-eating love grass nonexistent. But scoring well depends on the ability to strike accurate approach shots and a facility with the flat stick. Missing the greens means descending into cavernous greenside bunkers more often than not, as there is an average of almost two per hole. Hitting the green is no guarantee of par either. "If you don't land on the right section of the green, two-putting can be a chore," offers Walker. A wonderful example of such is on the par-5 second hole, 500 yards from the tips, and fronted by an ample lagoon. Beyond different levels, it's as though there are actually separate platforms on this green, separated by deep swales. End up on the nether side of the flag here and three putts

will be the standard, if not the minimum.

This isn't to imply that Crooked Oaks is a benign pastureland until it's time to start plumb bobbing your putts. The yardage tops out at a relatively petite 6,750. But the course and slope rating of 73 and 139 are not only testament to the inherent difficulty, but also a mirror image of the quantifying numbers at Ocean Winds, generally believed to be a much sterner overall test of the game.

This isn't to imply that Crooked Oaks is a benign pastureland until it's time to start plumb bobbing your putts.

Though the tee-to-green challenge isn't as unrelenting as exists on its sister track, there are a few shots that make a player stand and deliver. There's virtually nothing in the way of forced carries off the tee, but several approach shots must be launched up and over trouble to reach the greens. Besides the aforementioned second hole, the tricky par-4 fourth is not only home to "the" crooked oak on Crooked Oaks, but also a ball-swallowing, off-limits, environmentally sensitive area guarding a puzzlingly difficult green. The 10th is a longer par 4, just over or under 400 yards in length, depending on whether a player chooses to play from the tips or penultimate markers. For the vast majority of non-bombers taking to the links, the long iron or utility wood approach shot needs to float over a broad lagoon guarding the green. Just like on the 18th, where the water encroaches insidiously on the right to doom a sliced approach shot, there's a bulkhead bracketing the water hazard. It adds drama, and provides an unmistakable visual cue from the fairway. But it doesn't make the shot at hand any easier.

Inaccurate references are often made to treeless courses like the adjacent Ocean Winds as "links" or "links style" tracks. The irony here is that while Crooked Oaks is a parkland style, tree-lined course, the routing is absolutely links-like. The first eight holes head in a southwest direction with very little variation. The par-3 ninth is literally the turning point, and the remaining holes head almost straight back in the opposite direction, with the final hole directly paralleling the first. The predominant wind shifts depending on the season, but if it's at a player's back heading out, rest assured it'll be in their face making the turn for home, or vice versa.

Real estate is the raison d'être at virtually every golf development in the Southeast, and Seabrook Island is no exception. While the condo complexes and modern dwellings offer a stark contrast to the playing fields at Ocean Winds, Crooked Oaks is something different entirely. The housing here is ever present and innocuous concurrently. As the name implies, the course is bracketed with trees. The housing presence is relatively constant, but also set back from the playing corridors, low profile in nature and well camouflaged in some instances by tree cover and vegetation. Concentrating on the demands of the course and the game at hand relegates the real estate component to an afterthought, which is exactly how it should be.

At a glance, Crooked Oaks would seem to take a backseat to its older sibling. Ocean Winds has the lyrical moniker, the championship legacy, the more dramatic routing. But first impressions can be deceiving. In its own way, this Trent Jones beauty is every bit the equal of the adjacent golf course, with challenges and a unique beauty of its own. In tandem, the courses at Seabrook Island make for a powerfully compelling one-two punch.

Number 8, Par 4

Essay: Deterioration

*I*t used to be I had a puncher's chance of breaking 80 most every time I played, but now it's oftentimes a death struggle to break 90. Why? What went wrong?

It's a sad irony, because the reason I became a golf writer was because the game was an endless fascination, and by recreational standards my abilities were well above average. Now it's just an endless frustration, and I continue to sink further and further into mediocrity. For the briefest possible moment, my handicap stood at 5. There was a longer dalliance at 6, a steady relationship at 7, and several happy years as an 8 or 9. Now, as the magic number continues to float inexorably towards the teens, the single-digit standard once taken for granted seems as unreachable and far off as Pluto.

Although my basic fundamentals have always had more flaws than a department store diamond ...

I'm quite certain as to why this happened. A copious and obsessive record keeper, several years ago I was stopped dead in my tracks by a bravura decision to tote up all the sub-80 rounds I'd conjured. (A brief aside: There must be a technical term for those who track life's minutia in journals, calendars or spreadsheets, but busy with business and family I've yet to make time to pursue a degree in psychiatry.) When I added up these individual moments of relative golfing brilliance, the total stood at about 170. At the time, I was shooting in the 70's several dozen times a season, and foolishly thought ahead to the milestone accomplishment of my 200th round below 80.

Since that ill-fated accounting, the thin stream of sub-80 rounds I occasionally enjoyed slowed to a trickle, then a drip. Now it's a veritable Chinese Water Torture, as the seasons, even our household clocks change more often that I walk off the final green in 79 blows or less.

There are of course technical reasons for the denouement of my game. Although my basic fundamentals have always had more flaws than a department store diamond, proficiency chipping and pitching the ball has often made up for the 95 percent of the greens missed in regulation. Now that single saving grace has abandoned me as well. But to my mind it's the metaphysical reasons and not the technical ones that have precipitated this shocking demise.

A brief analogy: Decades ago someone close to me had a happy and fruitful home life, though struggled to find business success. Eventually he made his mark, and while earning the admiration of his industry peers and a modest fortune besides, he ended up divorced and with a broken family. Several years later and remarried once more, he suffered a serious heart attack. Though he recovered nicely, is remarried yet again and continues to enjoy professional success, the lesson he inadvertently imparted during this period rings true today. It's awfully hard to have it all.

One of my very good golf buddies once asked me a profound question. "Would you rather have this golf-writing career, or be a scratch player?" I gave his query a thorough mulling over and later replied that I'd rather be a writer. The rationale is simple: Even Tiger Woods is rarely satisfied with his daily performance. If you're scratch you hope to be a "plus 1," and if you're "plus 1" you dream of being "plus 2." In that long-ago heady heyday of mid-single digits, I aspired to go lower still, setting my sights on a 3 handicap. Now I'd give up Budweiser and my Big Bertha besides for a precarious hold on a 9, so really it's all relative.

Even Tiger Woods is rarely satisfied with his daily performance.

I'm still counting those sub-80 rounds to this day, but suffice it to say I don't need a calculator to keep up with the flurry. Eventually, I hope to get all the way to the mythical 200, and if and when it happens, the belated celebration will be even sweeter. Though the game continues to provide more aggravation than elation, I don't foresee a scenario that involves quitting cold turkey when reaching the long-awaited milestone. I'll just do what I should have done long ago and quit counting. I'll be sure to limit my future tallying just to the strokes taken that particular day. Usually that number alone is quite high enough.

Ocean Winds

SEABROOK ISLAND RESORT

Number 13, Par 4

This book might become a New York Times best-seller. Don't laugh, it could happen, although the odds are just slightly longer than this correspondent someday donning the unsightly green jacket hall-marking a Masters champion. But even if this book were to suddenly set the publishing world on fire, it wouldn't matter a lick. Because Charleston, unlike other regional hot spots like Myrtle Beach, Hilton Head and Pinehurst, will always be an extremely underrated golf destination. And in at least one opinion, anyway, no single destination in the region is more underrated than Seabrook Island.

Serenely beautiful Seabrook, with its small-town feel, is adjacent to Kiawah Island. They are scarcely separated by Captain Sam's Inlet and the Kiawah River, a combination of stream and marshland that fluctuates with the tides. Beaches and boating, kayaking and sunset cruising, even surfside horse-back rides are among the chief attractions here. Easy to understand, when you're fortunate enough to be where land turns to sand and then sea. But golf is no afterthought, and the pair of courses on property are both excellent.

Willard Byrd's Ocean Winds is the more notable of the two course offerings at Seabrook. This 6,765-yard nature walk is a course of plenty: plenty of trouble, plenty of scenery, plenty of shot-making challenge, plenty of wildlife. Though it's rarely mentioned in the same breath as some of the marquee venues in the immediate vicinity and elsewhere in the region, it should be. Ocean Winds is undoubtedly one of the staunchest and most scenic golf adventures in the Lowcountry, the inward nine particularly.

"Ocean Winds is a terrific test," says Beth Daniel, the LPGA Hall of Fame member and native Charlestonian. "It's tight off the tee, and winds its way through sand dunes throughout. The greens are small, and the elements play a large factor because several holes are exposed to the seaside breezes. It's a links-style course - very few trees, but lots of native grasses and sand dunes abounding."

"Ocean Winds is a terrific test," says Beth Daniel, the LPGA Hall of Fame member and native Charlestonian.

Daniel is correct, as the difficulty factor can be distilled down to four simple words: narrow fairways, smallish greens. Some of the fairways look no wider than a driveway. But that's partially due to visual intimidation and psychological pressure, because the love grass and lagoons loom close at hand, constricting the playing fields. The opening nine is more of a parkland setting and offers some breathing room, although one might be inhaling and exhaling among the trees. But the second half of the course offers limited bailout room for wayward tee shots, and the short grass oasis we're all looking for seems to shrink considerably, at least in the mind's eye.

This anxiety factor isn't limited to typical resort players or those with hefty handicaps. When the South Carolina Open was contested here in 1998, the winning score was even par over three rounds. Director of Golf Alan Walker has some 15 years of tenure, and explains why the best pros in the region couldn't get into red figures. "The participants were wary of all the trouble to be found out here, and because the course isn't overly long, many chose to play conservatively from the tee. But laying back with a fairway wood or long iron reduces the odds of hitting our small greens," says the native Mississippian. "A strong player has to take controlled risks out here to shoot low numbers, and try and bomb the occasional tee shot to have a short iron into the green. It wasn't even that windy during the tournament, but the players were having a difficult time finding fairways, regardless."

The picture-book example of this sensibility might be found on the 14th, a deadly little diamond of a par 4, just 330 yards short. Here from the tee box on the easternmost point of the property is the closest a player actually gets to the ocean. The surf might be pounding but it's impossible to tell because there looks to be a quarter mile of vegetation between the golf course and beach. Hearts will undoubtedly be pounding, though, because there are out of bounds, bunkers and waving grasses framing the landing zone. The approach on this "puppy leg" left (it's too small to call it an actual dogleg) is to a small, tilting green protected by palm trees, sandy scrub vegetation and a snaking waste bunker encircling the rear. Other than that, it's a piece of cake.

Only a kennel has more doglegs than Ocean Winds, as the architect had to route the holes in serpentine fashion amid the existing dunes and grasses. Speaking of animals, the course is a certified member of the Audubon Cooperative Sanctuary Program. So it's a bird sanctuary as well as a Byrd sanctuary. There's a rookery near the fourth green that teems with ornithological life during the warm-weather months. Hitting the green on the minefield-laden, par-3 15th is a chore, and once safely aboard, the tilted putting surface isn't the only reason players won't be watching many birdie putts diving in the hole. That's because one's concentration is sapped watching the pelicans diving for fish in the lagoon just behind the green. Sure, we've all seen plenty of fancy birds and scary gators in our Charleston golf travels. But what about bobcats? One might encounter a trio of these slightly fierce "kitty-carnivores" lazing in the sun on the 18th tee, looking on dispassionately, as relaxed as any fat cat could be. Easy to understand, as they don't have to deal with the ferocious finisher - 400 yards, with water guarding the green both left and right.

Only a kennel has more doglegs than Ocean Winds.

Some might be shell-shocked, but other players will be steeled for this final drive, having run a gauntlet of one-shot holes that collectively might be the most troublesome in the region. The fifth is almost 180 yards from the penultimate markers, with water right and tree trouble left. The eighth is more straightforward but longer, with a ball-eating bunker right of the green. The 12th green is fronted by another massive sand cavern, and simply put, the aforementioned 15th offers no room to miss in any direction.

The 16th deserves quick mention as well. This is an eminently reachable par 5, less than 500 yards from the tips and some 470 from the penultimate markers. But once again, a talented player needs to weigh the risk of blasting a drive down a narrow, crowned fairway with environmentally sensitive areas (i.e., lateral hazards) both right and left. A fade will bounce right and a hook will bound left. Whichever the direction, the end result is the same: a penalty stroke. Cerebral players often opt to bunt the ball into play with something less than the whipping stick, and plod their way to a safe par or perhaps up-and-down birdie. There are plans in place to flatten the landing area and reduce the crowned effect of the fairway, which is a fine idea, because as currently configured, 16 definitely needs a bit of sweetening.

Golf course critique is most often done from the ground level. Discussions of greens, fairways, vegetation, water hazards and bunkers predominate.

Golf course critique is most often done from the ground level. Discussions of greens, fairways, vegetation, water hazards and bunkers predominate. But no thorough observation of Ocean Winds would be complete without at least a brief mention of the unique atmospheric conditions that provide a quality of light only occasionally seen in the golf world. Traversing the property, on a cloudless morning in particular, the course is bathed in an unusual lambent light. Although a golfer never actually gets within a stone's throw (or a crushed driver, for that matter) of the beach itself, the whole ambience of the course is "beachy." It has to do with the dearth of trees, the modern villas close at hand and the waving love grass and fescue, among other qualities. Whatever the scientific reasons may be, the fact is that the refulgence adds yet another attractive element to Ocean Winds. With apologies in advance for the pun, it provides another reason as to why this course is one of Charleston's most illuminating golf experiences.

Number 15, Par 3

WILD DUNES RESORT

Number 7, Par 4

A wise guy golf pro, someone in the mold of Lee Trevino or Sam Snead, once used a colorful description for a tight driving hole. "I'm not saying it was narrow," cracked the Merry Mex, Slamming Sammy or someone just as irreverent. "But we had to walk the fairways single file."

That same sentiment kept running through my head while touring Tom Fazio's Harbor Course, the little brother to the more-esteemed Links Course at Wild Dunes, on the Isle of Palms north of Charleston. The "single file" line is an exaggeration, but at the same time, you couldn't get Craig Stadler, "Lumpy" Herron, Ed Fiori and John Daly walking four abreast without someone getting their feet wet in a water hazard or cracking a knee against an out-

of-bounds stake.

The Harbor Course, named because of its proximity to the Intracoastal Waterway and Wild Dunes Yacht Harbor, is tougher than shoe leather, mostly because it's tighter than a scuba suit. Pick a vivid analogy of your own choosing.

It's narrower than a dorm-room bed, skinnier than Paris Hilton after a juice fast. "The marshes and vegetation encroach very closely onto the playing corridors," admits the architect. "The course runs north to south, and the foliage and undergrowth bracket the fairways." It's scenic, interesting both visually and from a playability standpoint. It has a nice variance of holes from tame (a couple of par 3's and short par 5's) to terrifying (the closing trio). But over and over, the golf course demands precision from both the tee and the fairway. It's a ball eater at minimum, though many would categorize it a bit more colorfully as a "ball with another verb" instead. Are you with me, Buster?

It's narrower than a dorm-room bed, skinnier than Paris Hilton after a juice fast.

The main reason for the tapered nature of the terrain is because of the footprint of the course. If an average golf course is the size of an average man's footprint, then a massively scaled course, the best neighborhood example might be Charleston National, has a footprint like Sasquatch. By contrast, the Harbor Course is more like a baby shoe, the kind grandmothers might've bronzed and put on display. "The acreage we had to work with was truncated. It's more akin to the size and scope of courses that were built at the turn of the last century," continues Fazio. "We routed holes in the upland areas that were available between the marshes and water features. In that way, it was like a puzzle because we would link holes together where the land allowed us to construct them practically." To be a bit more specific, while the total course acreage might be somewhat in line with a normal course, there are untold acres of vegetation, marshes, lagoons, etc., so the playing field proper, where you can actually land the golf ball, is somewhat smaller than most courses.

The golf course is cleverly routed through a vibrant series of neighborhoods throughout the upscale Wild Dunes Resort.

The golf course is cleverly routed through a vibrant series of neighborhoods throughout the upscale Wild Dunes Resort. Lowcountry golfers are certainly used to playing through real estate subdivisions, as it's the modus operandi throughout much of the Southeast. But the Harbor Course takes this sensibility to an entirely different level. Players pass by municipal buildings and through different neighborhoods as they chase the ball around slender swatches of green grass. Road crossings are a given, and there are several instances where the cart path melds into the roadway itself, and the golfer shares space democratically with any vehicle or bicycle that

might happen along concurrently. The designer explains that one of the holes at the southern end of the property was actually a grass runway for a tiny airport before it became part of the golf course. This all sounds as distracting as a circus, but the underlying fact is this: The Harbor Course is, disruptions aside, a compelling golf experience.

Playing 6,360 yards from the tips, this par 70 has several defining characteristics. The front nine is a par 36 that is a full 500 yards longer than the back, with a par of 34. Owing to the abridged nature of the terrain, Fazio designed six par 3's in his routing. But this is no "executive course," not by a long stretch, if you'll excuse the pun. The eighth and ninth are back-to-back par 5's, each better than 560 yards in length. The closing holes are a pair of two-shot monsters, 450 yards on average, with marsh trouble in almost every direction. Members of the professional staff like to say the closers are the two hardest back-to-back holes in the world. If that strikes you as a bit of an exaggeration, please reserve judgment until you're standing on the penultimate tee. "I think the difficulty of the closing holes is justified," says the architect. "There are a number of short or medium-length par 4's preceding the finale, and the rugged nature of the finishers brings the course into total balance. It's like Philadelphia's Merion, in a way, which also has some easier or shorter par 4's before concluding with very tough holes around the famous quarry." Far be it for this correspondent to question the opinion of the man known as "America's Greatest Living Architect." But comparing classic, elegant Merion with this modernly eccentric amalgamation requires the imagination of, well, America's Greatest Living Architect.

Another oddity: The haul between the fourth and fifth holes is close to five minutes in length. By golf cart, mind you. Anyone foolhardy enough to walk will grind down an entire set of Softspikes between green and tee. The return journey from the 12th to the 13th is another marathon journey, though not quite as lengthy. The major reason for the eclectic configuration of the Harbor Course is because of the onslaught of Hurricane Hugo, the unwelcome visitor that altered the area golf landscape indelibly in 1989, four years after the course was constructed. The holes nearest the resort, the first four and final five, are originals. The middle nine had to be reworked and rerouted after the storm hit, and offer more of a target sensibility than exists elsewhere.

The "hit straight or die" mentality is distilled to its essence at the pint-sized 11th, only 145 yards from the tips.

Cart commutes aren't the only length required at the Harbor Course. The sixth is just 380 yards in total, but the tee ball needs to angle over what seems like an ocean of vegetation to find a narrow fairway. The approach doesn't get any wider, and the green is pocket-sized, as are most on the property. Without sheer length as a detriment to scoring, there is some visual deception at work. From the back tees especially, as the 5,900-yard forward markers are much more straightforward, one might be inclined to say, "It looks like a nice hole, all it's missing is a fairway," a time or two. But the fact is that the fairways are there, just camouflaged by foliage. In that way, it's the antithesis of the resort course it's designed to be, because a first-timer will be scratching his head, often wondering precisely in which direction his tee shot needs to soar.

The "hit straight or die" mentality is distilled to its essence at the pint-sized 11th, only 145 yards from the tips. But simply put, there is nowhere to miss. Left or right of the green, running the length of the hole is a lateral-hazard marsh. It's short and simple, but intimidating because the error margin is negligible.

All this required accuracy generally sends most Wild Dunes members to the more forgiving Links Course. Resort guests play the Harbor as much as the Links, which is partially a function of a lesser greens fee. Suffice it to say that the two courses afford entirely different playing experiences and price points.

"If every course around the world was as narrow as the Harbor Course, golf would be an even more difficult game," concludes Tom Fazio. "But because the Links Course was so successful, the developers wanted us to build a second course on property. We built a fine course with the land available to us, and the Harbor is very distinctive because of its unique challenges." While his original effort at Wild Dunes garners most of the attention and accolades, the Harbor Course completes the yin and yang of one of greater Charleston's best-loved golf destinations.

Number 13, Par 3

ESSAY: GOLF - THE MOST DANGEROUS GAME

So golf is for wimps, you say. It's not a sport for true athletes. Well, on certain levels it's a hard point to argue. Let's face it, the physiques belonging to the likes of Tim Herron, John Daly, Craig Stadler, and to be totally unbiased from a gender perspective, former U.S. Women's Open champions Laura Davies and Hilary Lunke don't remind anyone of Greek statuary.

Golf is a dangerous game, my friend, and I know it for a fact.

But what defines a true athlete, anyway? Skill, dexterity, ability to perform under pressure and hand/eye coordination are some of the criteria. How about dealing with injuries? Don't laugh, there's more to fear on the golf course than a sunburn, hay fever and blisters from ill-fitting spikes.

Golf is a dangerous game, my friend, and I know it for a fact. Let me share a trio of vignettes with you. Three different seasons, three different reasons, three different locales, all proving that golf can be a lot more harrowing than the simple walk in the park critics sometimes imply.

Western Massachusetts, early 90s.

A misfire off the tee box almost caused catastrophic injury to one of my best pals. I was aiming at 12:00, trying to bisect the fairway of a tree-lined par 4. Happy Jack was standing safely, we both presumed, at 10:30 or 11:00, perhaps 20 yards ahead of the tee box at the ball washer. I pull-hooked a crushing liner that hit him in the upper pectoral muscle. The time disparity between impact of club to ball and then ball to body bordered on instantaneous. He leapt off the ground in shock and pain, a vertical leap the world hadn't seen since Michael Jordan was a Carolina Tarheel. Had the ball struck elsewhere? In the throat? The temple? The eye, forehead, or horror of horrors, below the belt? Never mind the last person, it likely would've been the last golf shot I ever struck.

After a solid five minutes of writhing histrionics, Happy Jack tried to continue playing, but couldn't get the club back anywhere near parallel. He chipped and putted for a few holes, then just putted, and eventually motored back to the clubhouse for a six-pack to go.

That night we were at a party, and that bruise, with dimple imprints clearly visible on the skin, turned more colors than a Hawaiian sunset. Things turned out okay, I'm happy to report, and several years later, my friend doubled the size of his family, becoming the father of twin boys. I'm so very glad that stray missile of mine, if it had to hit anywhere, hit well above the zipper.

... that bruise, with dimple imprints clearly visible on the skin, turned more colors than a Hawaiian sunset.

Northern Utah, just past the millennium.

I blame the teenagers I was paired with. Those two mumble-mouths never told me I was at the blue tee markers when I crushed a beautiful drive right down the pipeline. They knew I was playing the championship markers, and when I walked off the tee, I noticed the tee box I meant to hit from was 30 yards farther back and at an angle to the fairway. I stalked back, re-hit, and delivered a wondrous slice to the parallel fairway of this forgettable municipal track. My poor victim was addressing what must have been her third shot as the ball veered towards her like a heat-seeking missile.

"Fore!" I screamed as loudly as possible, but before the echo died out, my offending Top Flite conked her squarely in the melon. Down she went in a heap, and the imprint of her fall attested to how quickly and drastically she went from upright to prone.

Self-preservation is our most basic instinct, and as the adrenaline started coursing through my body, I urgently said to my teenage companions, "You guys heard me yell 'Fore,' right?" They nodded in assent, and I took off across the fairway. The husband had already loaded his prostrate wife into the golf cart. I sped towards them, but he was speeding away towards the clubhouse. I yelled across, "I'm really so sorry. I yelled out a warning as loudly as I could."

He angrily replied, "She's bleeding like a stuck pig!"

I went to my ball, which was in a nice lie, all things considered. I hit a utility wood onto the green, but then the golf gods caught up with me. I three-putted from 20 feet for bogey.

Coastal Georgia, late 90s.

I had the phenomenally bad luck of engaging an

inch-thick tree root in a little game of "chicken," which was a mismatch from the opening bell. This wasn't your standard tree root, lying there plainly visible. Had that been the case, I might have declared an unplayable lie and taken a penalty drop away from the root. Or at least would have attempted a thin defensive shot, holding the club lightly and attempting to play the ball out laterally. Neither of these options was a consideration, because this root was as devious as they come, a real predator. Lying there perfectly camouflaged by a thin layer of autumn leaves, awaiting an innocent and unlucky victim. I took out a 3-iron and attempted to reach the green, 190 yards from where I stood. To make matters worse, my golf swing is rarely compared to that of Fred Couples or Ernie Els, they of the long and languid swings, swings that look like they are taking place under water. Mine by comparison starts quickly, picks up speed in the middle and ends in a hurried lurch. The iron came down, met that damned root and stopped dead. It was like kicking a brick wall in sandals.

It was like kicking a brick wall in sandals.

My right hand vibrated with pain. Walking up the fairway in a daze, I realized all too well there had been some serious damage inflicted upon my dominant hand.

In the aftermath, I was x-rayed, bone scanned, and re-x-rayed. I used ice, heat, ultrasound, acupuncture and something called iontophersis. Assisted at various junctures by an orthopedist, an osteopath, a masseuse, a hand surgeon, a physical therapist and a Chinese healer. Note: don't believe anyone who tells you that acupuncture hurts a little. They are wrong. It hurts plenty!

The injury eventually ran its course. Months later I walked to the first tee with a brand-new attitude, one that was supposed to last the rest of my life, but in truth, disappeared with the first triple bogey. Fat shots or thin, slices or hooks, shots that are stiff and shots that are sculled. I still savor them all, knowing that my hand and wrist now hold up at the moment of impact. And one last thing. Arbor Day is now at the top of my list of least-favorite holidays.

Links Course

WILD DUNES RESORT

Number 18, Par 5

Pardon the confusion, but the golf schedule has been even more hectic than usual in the making of this book. The courses and their creators are starting to jumble in the mind just a bit. Was it Pete Dye who gave us the Links Course at Wild Dunes? Or was it Tom Fazio who produced Harbour Town?

No, it's not as if the courses are identical twins, or even kissing cousins. But in repeated forays to Charleston, it was only natural to compare and contrast all the courses being discovered initially with the venues I've grown to know so well on Hilton Head, which was my main subject in a prior book.

In this opinion, no course in greater Charleston has as much resemblance to Harbour Town Golf Links, Hilton Head's marquee destination, as the estimable

Links Course at Wild Dunes resort. There are similarities in the greens, the routing and the finish, among others. Another symmetry is that these two designs were the first to truly catapult their respective creators to national prominence. But before a more detailed analysis ensues, it's instructive to compare these modern classics on another level.

Harbour Town's Charleston-area doppelganger in terms of status and iconography is now the Ocean Course on Kiawah Island. There can be little argument that these two venues are "the" places to play, the signature courses for a visiting golfer to tackle. Furthermore, they both enjoy legacies as pro-golf bastions, the seminal Ryder Cup at Kiawah in 1991 and the ongoing annual PGA Tour stop on Hilton Head.

But the massive, sprawling Ocean Course is more of an organic golf experience - it's wild and wooly, the ambience almost like golf on another planet or at least golf in the British Isles.

By contrast, both the Links Course, which remains more than 25 years after creation one of the very few destination golf venues in town, and Harbour Town are literally more civilized. Both have thoughtful routings requiring shots that must be shaped off the tee. But the swaths of fairway are cut between road crossings, near condos and showpiece homes. It's a testament to the architectural genius of their designers that the delightful golf experiences supersede the distractions of everyday life that surround it.

"Without the buildings, you wouldn't have golf at Wild Dunes," says Tom Fazio flatly. "The course and the development go hand in hand, particularly during that time frame in the early 80's, when the course was being finished. It's no surprise that there's a lot of real estate surrounding it." Fazio prefers to focus on the outstanding routing he envisioned - counter-clockwise on the front and serpentine on the back, taking full advantage of the unusual topography. "When I first came to Wild Dunes in the late 70's, the management team had already devised a golf course routing. But in my opinion, the golf course they had planned didn't take full advantage of the site. I suggested we move the course from the center of the property farther northward, nearer the ocean. I realized right away that, if we located it properly, it would immediately gain attention as one of the best new courses in the country."

> *But the massive, sprawling Ocean Course is more of an organic golf experience - it's wild and wooly, the ambience almost like golf on another planet or at least golf in the British Isles.*

The management group was skeptical of the proposal made by an architect who was just then breaking away from a long-standing partnership with his uncle, George Fazio, and going out on his own. Looking at the staked-out markers for greens, fairways and tees, they wondered how a course could be routed through the dunes in such an intimate fashion. "They thought it was too dune-like, hilly and full of ravines. But I thought it was a tremendous site," continues the architect. The finished product, the more spectacular back nine, with its seaside finish in particular, won its creator national acclaim. For a long while, the Links Course was firmly ensconced in the worldwide top-100 lists, and was the project that jump-started Fazio's solo design career.

"Our members and resort guests still clamor to play the course," says former Director of Golf Marty Mikesell. "They love the views, the up-and-down nature of the topography, the dunes. They also know it's where Tom Fazio's career really began.

And many of our well-traveled visitors who've played marquee Fazio courses all over comment that the Links is still one of his very best designs."

> *"Many of our well-traveled visitors who've played marquee Fazio courses all over comment that the Links is still one of his very best designs."*

Rather petite by modern standards at just 6,700 yards from the tips, what makes the course difficult is its general tightness off the tee. Everything is relative, and compared to "little brother," the overly constricted Harbor Course elsewhere on the property, the Links is as open as a desolate Nebraskan prairie. But comparisons aside, it's a course that must be tiptoed, tread softly upon. Brute force, "long and wrong," won't cut it. There are overhanging limbs, encroaching cart paths, marshes, water hazards and skinny, sinister white stakes punctuating the landscape, delineating the inbounds playing fields from the adjacent backyards. The course isn't any longer on the back, but it gets a bit bigger. Fairways thankfully widen. The greens, which on the front are often as small and undistinguished as Harbour Town's, grow in both size and tilt.

Truthfully, the Links is defined on the inward journey. The opening nine holes are pleasant enough, punctuated by the intriguing fifth. This reachable par 5 of 500 yards culminates with a bunker-guarded, raised green, angled to the right and tucked behind a large mound. The flagstick must be more than 12 feet tall so players can see the target from the fairway below. Not even Yao Ming, Tim Duncan or any other NBA behemoth would be able to keep the flag from flapping in the breeze while tending the pin.

This Isle of Palms resort is well named, though, because the second half of the course is both wild and often routed through the dunes. The drama begins in earnest on the 10th tee. An uphill par 4 of about 330 yards, it features a dramatically rolling, staircase fairway, framed by a lone tree standing sentinel on the right flank. It's a small miracle to land in the short grass and find a flat lie for the short approach. The 11th is slightly longer at 375 yards, but is condensed nonetheless by an elevated tee box, assuming one can fit the tee shot between the dunes that line both sides of the fairway. It's another stunner. The 190-yard 12th, which might be the most memorable and visually intimidating holes on the property, looks like it was airlifted from Scotland. Framed by long native grasses, this downhill shot to a smallish green is no easy three. Too bad the Scottish Highlands feel disappears as a player drives towards the green, realizing the hole is adjacent to a busy thoroughfare in the resort.

The Links, no such arriviste, was born in the dying days of disco.

The housing ambience, the mostly elfin greens, the shot-shaping requirements and the seaside finish are all reminiscent of Harbour Town. Until a few years ago, there was an additional, regrettable similarity, but that issue has been addressed down on Hilton Head. Prior to the course renovation in 2000, Harbour Town had a tremendous disparity between the championship and penultimate markers, almost 800 yards of difference. That situation's been rectified, and instead of being shoehorned at 6,000 yards or stretched to the limits at 6,900, reasonably skilled players can now choose markers in the 6,500-yard range. Not so at the Links though, where there still exists a 600-yard disparity between the black and white markers. If 6,700 yards is too much golf course, then the next best option as currently configured is just a tad over 6,100. The logical explanation has to do with pace-of-play issues. Moving most folks forward to the truncated white tees keeps things moving more briskly, which is never a bad idea. But regardless, a set of markers placed at 6,400 yards would be a welcome addition, and allow many more players to choose the most appropriate distance for their skill level.

Only Charleston's golf courses circa 1990 and beyond can be discussed meaningfully without at least a passing reference to Hurricane Hugo. The Links, no such arriviste, was born in the dying days of disco. It was almost dealt a death blow itself about a decade after creation, when Hugo the Horrible blew through town on the first day of autumn in 1989. With winds of 138 m.p.h. and a 20-foot storm surge on top of astronomically high tides, Wild Dunes fared worse than most.

It was the strongest storm in some 35 years, and had a paralyzing, albeit temporary effect on the area's golf industry. "Lots of the trees and vegetation that were framing the golf holes were lost," explains Fazio, the man generally known as America's greatest living architect. "After awhile, the vegetation returns or is replanted. In certain instances, the course might've improved, because you're always hesitant to remove mature plant species in the building process, but sometimes Mother Nature takes care of things for you." Thousands of pines were lost, although the oak trees withstood the storm. "The felled trees that were on the east and south side of the playing areas helped improve the air circulation and allowed more sunlight, which ultimately improved the course conditions."

"The reputation of the course is intact to this day. It's one of the finest courses in the Charleston area, and for that matter, the entire Southeast coast."

Regardless of the inevitability of storms, the proliferation of housing as more and more people flock to Charleston's beachfront communities and islands, the growth and increased competition in both the resort and daily-fee golf market, Fazio concludes saying, "The reputation of the course is intact to this day. It's one of the finest courses in the Charleston area, and for that matter, the entire Southeast coast. Wild Dunes will always be a special place for me." And the signature Links Course remains a special golf experience for all who choose to visit and confront its unique and memorable challenges.

SECTION II

Charleston National

Number 4, Par 4

Charleston National's position in the top tier of the city's daily-fee offerings is unassailable. Hole after hole is a thoughtful challenge, and certain areas of the course are set on some of the most visually stimulating terrain in the region. But the Charleston National that members and visitors enjoy today, because of circumstances far beyond the reach of man, is an entirely different entity than what was originally conceived.

Nineteen eighty-nine's Hurricane Hugo wasn't kind to the city or its burgeoning golf industry in general, but the impact of this hellacious storm was arguably more destructive for Charleston National than it was for any other golf venue in the area. The storm actually hit shortly before the Grand Opening week of what was supposed to be an exclusively private venue.

"When I first went back there after the storm, the work of art that I had created was still in place," reminisces architect Rees Jones. "But the frame, in other words the trees, was gone. Fortunately the frame has been reestablished over time."

"Charleston National is a course that I originally compared to my design at Haig Point, farther south on South Carolina's Daufuskie Island," continues Jones, referring to his award-winning work near Hilton Head. "The setting was phenomenal up in Mount Pleasant, not far from Isle of Palms. When Hurricane Hugo hit just as the course was being readied to open, it was devastating. A 15-foot storm surge went across the property, and 7,000 trees snapped like twigs."

Carlyle Altman was the superintendent at the time, and was actually on the property when the storm hit. He reported that the eye of the storm came across the golf course, and the vacuum effect sucked the water off with such force that the pine trees went down like toothpicks, although many of the oaks survived. "Believe it or not, the course was playable again three weeks later, thanks to the drainage and the grading we had done," says Jones.

"Now when you go back there you wouldn't even know that happened. It's still a natural golf course with a wonderful feel. There's still a significant marsh and wetland presence, and it's a darn good public golf course. It's really got that Lowcountry look. The extensive natural wetlands that are prevalent on the closing stretch of holes are home to an annual migration of wood storks, which is a huge plus."

The opening trio of holes at Charleston National makes for a taxing beginning. The first is a 400-yard par 4 constricted by vegetation and woods. A 150-yard par 3 to a narrow green completely surrounded by wetlands follows, and the next is a dogleg par 4 of 400 yards requiring a precision drive. It's not that the architect was looking to bludgeon a player from the get-go, it's just that the course routing was reconfigured after Hugo. These openers were supposed to be closers, the final three holes on the course, leading to magnificent views of Hamlin Sound and a grand clubhouse on the northeast point of the property. But the clubhouse was never built in that location. It was constructed elsewhere on the site, and instead there are a handful of high-dollar waterside mansions beyond the green at the third hole. Though there are some 700 homes surrounding the golf course, aside from these showpiece homes abutting the Sound, the residences are mostly a peripheral presence, at least early in the round. Through much of the outward nine, the course is parkland style, with scant resemblance to a typical golf-real estate development so common in this part of the world.

There are three distinct golf phases at Charleston National. The first four holes are marsh-side, and sniffing distance from the water. The course turns inland from there, and the succeeding nine holes are routed through the forest, albeit a thinner forest than originally anticipated. The final five are back among the wetlands again, and the bridge crossings and mile-long views of the Lowcountry make these the most memorable holes on the property. These finishing five are a radical departure from what came before. They offer the juxtaposition in routing style that makes this closing stretch unforgettable.

The golf course can be stretched to almost 7,100 yards in length, although most anyone will have all they can handle at 6,750 yards, with a sturdy 133 slope rating. Most of the length is compressed in the middle portion of the round. Almost 45 percent of the total yardage is contained in a six-hole stretch beginning on the brutal eighth hole, a 460-yard par 4 with a gaping pond awaiting any tee shot drifting right of the fairway. Three of the next four are par 5's, and Jones saved the best of these longest holes for last. The 12th is a take-no-prisoners, risk/reward hole with a wetland bisecting the fairway. Popcorn hitters will need to lay up behind the vegetation with their second shot, while those in possession of the heavy artillery can attempt a pair of mighty swipes to reach the green.

These longer holes precede a delightful crescendo among untold acres of golden marshland.

Number 14, Par 3

These longer holes precede a delightful crescendo among untold acres of golden marshland. The housing and woodlands are left behind as a series of narrow bridges wend their way between curving fairways. Though substantially shorter in length, the final holes are characterized by forced carries. The 15th is a bit tricky. It's only 370 yards long, but the marsh carry to find the canted fairway is close to 200 yards from the blue (or in this particular case, green) markers. The penultimate hole is perhaps the prettiest and most difficult hole on the property, a serenely isolated dogleg par 4 of 420 yards. The course concludes with a cute par 3 over even more wetlands. It's a fitting if slightly unorthodox end to a course whose strongest suit is its wide range of different aspects and playing characteristics.

Hugo dealt a paralyzing blow to Charleston National, but it wasn't a death blow. The rarified air surrounding the club dissipated with the maelstrom of the storm. What was to be the province of the privileged few moneyed golfers who were looking for yet another private club to join, now belongs to anyone willing to pony up the quite-reasonable greens fee. "I think the daily-fee players are fortunate to have access to a facility of this caliber," concludes the architect. "It's beautiful, challenging and has a nice feel to it. The public has benefited greatly by having access to this exceptional piece of land we turned into an excellent golf course. The pristine setting, with the long Lowcountry vistas, is a boon to the city's golfers and visiting players alike. Sometimes things just work out in a certain way."

Hugo dealt a paralyzing blow to Charleston National, but it wasn't a death blow.

On the one hand, it's a shame that the vision, the direction of the club, was altered so dramatically. But from an egalitarian perspective, it seems quite just that this estimable Rees Jones design is now available to all comers.

City of Charleston Golf Course

CHARLESTON, SOUTH CAROLINA

Number 12, Par 4

It's one of the great ironies of the Charleston golf scene. In a town replete with old-line, old-money clubs, nouveau dazzlers with six-figure initiation fees and glittering resort courses that attract vacationers from around the globe, one of the most interesting pedigrees belongs to the City of Charleston Golf Course. But in terms of its history, social significance and playing charactcristics, "The Muni" is anything but puny.

Trevor introduces himself on the first tee. He's an affable kid, a College of Charleston senior, capable of hitting it a long way, but in what direction is anyone's guess. His black T-shirt is inside out, much like his swing, which helps explain the distance he gets on an over-spinning tee ball on the rare occasion he catches it on the face. On the third tee, he nods in the direction of a 50-something black man putting on the second green, perhaps 30 yards to our left. "See that guy in the white cap? I've played with him at least 20 times, and I've never seen him shoot above par. He's amazing around the greens." The 20-something Virginian went on to explain that the short-game wizard's name was Prince, and that he was former military. Asked whether they set up games in advance, Trevor replied, "Never. We just seem to show up at about the same time in the afternoon, and that's when we hook up and play. That's how it is around here for most folks. They arrive as a single, maybe a twosome. Then they get paired up with one or two others, and head out."

Number 7, Par 4

It struck me that there probably wasn't a surfeit of opportunities in a city with Charleston's racially charged past where a seemingly carefree white collegian, one who exchanged his golf shoes for sandals on the final fairway, would find common ground with a meticulously dressed black veteran well over twice his age. But at The City Course, it's simply golf, not age, race, politics, couture or social class, that is the common denominator.

But at the city course, it's simply golf, not age, race, politics, couture or social class, that is the common denominator.

Beyond the social significance of the facility, the City of Charleston Golf Course is an appealing playing experience. In a sentence, the outward nine offers more of a strategic element, the inward nine more in the way of scenery. The course is less than five minutes from the Seth Raynor-designed Country Club of Charleston. Raynor died in 1926, three years prior to the Municipal's opening in 1929. J.M. Whitsitt, the chairman of the municipal golf course commission at the time, is credited with the thoughtful layout. There's no documentation that Raynor himself was ever involved in The City Course, but several of his design characteristics are evident.

Just 6,400 yards from the tips, and 6,150 from the white markers, sloped at 129 and 123 respectively, the course isn't about length. This one-time cotton plantation is a constricted piece of property, just 112 acres in total. It's bisected by the busy Maybank Highway and bordered by various side roads that were created as the community grew in around the course. Tee shots, occasionally approach shots, need to be shaped around overhanging trees to find the best angle to the greens. Many of these mostly shallow bunkers are located, as is often the case on Raynor courses, on either side of most every green. Just like at the nearby Country Club, landing the ball short of the target will usually leave a simple chip. But a drifting or hooking approach will almost always find the sand.

By no means does every bunker on the property resemble a kiddie wading pool. The approach to the wonderful par-5 seventh must carry over a "lion's mouth" bunker to a dramatically raised green. It brings to mind the similar hazard seen at the 16th of

the neighboring Country Club, fueling speculation that, though Raynor wasn't on the property during construction, a devotee was.

It's the cheapest thrill in town, golf-wise. If you're an out-of-towner, determined to use a buggy (though it's as good a walking course as any in the region) and play on a weekend morning, the tariff will be approaching $40. But as a weekday-afternoon, in-town ambler? Shockingly, he or she will get enough change from a ten-spot to purchase a beer or a Gatorade in the snack bar. Sounds like a bargain, but it's practically Pebble Beach-like in price compared to the four bits the city fathers charged for a round of 15 holes (the remaining three didn't open until the following year) back in the Roaring Twenties.

The bargain greens fees, like at municipal courses throughout the nation, help make golf affordable and available to the citizens of the region. But even as it approaches its 80th birthday, The City Course continues to evolve, and remains a work in progress. Antiquated remedies to old drainage issues come in the form of fairway-crossing trenches that were dug to ferry excess groundwater to adjacent ponds. Some tees and greens have shade problems created by the growth of 100-year-old oaks. But despite more than 60,000 rounds played annually, the turf grass is in reasonably good shape, and the green conditions are surprisingly consistent and smooth.

The bargain greens fees, like at municipal courses throughout the nation, help make golf affordable and available to the citizens of the region. But even as it approaches its 80th birthday, The City Course continues to evolve, and remains a work in progress.

Name architects like Rees Jones and Greenville's John LaFoy have rendered their opinion after inspecting The City Course while visiting Charleston. Both cautioned against changing the inherent character of the routing. They suggested that improvements and upgrades are necessary, as is the case with virtually all early-century courses, but wholesale changes would alter the makeup of this intriguing, throwback design.

Running parallel to the Maybank Highway at both the commencement and conclusion of the inward nine, the course and its surroundings are bustling with activity of all stripes. The traffic hurtling by dictates nets in place to protect windshields from wicked hooks and slices. Not exactly a walk in the park. But when the course turns perpendicularly from the through road, towards the Stono River early in the back nine, a different, more peaceable sensation ensues. The 12th and 13th holes in particular, a modest pair of par 4's, are set back among the vegetation, closer to the water than anywhere else on property. It's a welcome respite.

Number 12, Par 4

The direction of the holes is less important than the direction of the facility itself. After a long period of relative dormancy, Herb Whetsell, a police force major with more than 30 years of experience in city matters, was brought in as general manager in 2000. "We welcome everyone to our course," he says earnestly. "Seniors, kids, people of all races, ages and ability level. We want to offer quality golf at an affordable price."

One reason for the newly implemented hands-on attitude: In the past, the city subcontracted much of the course activities to outsiders - the snack bar, pro shop, driving range, etc. Now they control the whole operation, and stand to benefit greatly by increasing the quality of the entire golf experience, while reap-

ing the benefits of a burnished reputation and increased desirability. The city fathers are starting to understand the value of their sole golf amenity. Recent enhancements are evident and expert opinions have been solicited for future plans.

"We're no different from other city-owned recreation facilities, be they parks, baseball diamonds or soccer fields," continues Whetsell. "We must show our profitability to the city in the form of programs and access." Improvements to that end include a lighting installation on the driving range for evening practice sessions, the implementation of junior tees measuring 3,600 yards and scholarship programs for younger city golfers.

"The Muni" will never become a city landmark like Fort Sumter, the Battery or Rainbow Row. It doesn't attract the same level of golf-tourist traffic from out-of-towners, either, and won't until Kiawah, Wild Dunes and Seabrook Island hang "Going out of Business" signs on their respective front gates. But just because golfers don't arrive in Charleston specifically to play The City Course, it doesn't mean they don't happen along to give it a try, often more than once. Its price and proximity are salient selling points, considering the region's marquee-resort destinations are exponentially more expensive and much further afield. And because of its long history and "come one, come all" attitude, there's the type of rich ambience that simply doesn't exist at a resort facility. It's the type of place where old-timers sit on the porch telling colorful tales of "back in the day," and golfers of all abilities and backgrounds intermingle casually with different genders and races.

As is the case with all golf facilities built during the golden age of golf-course architecture, physical improvements to the facility are ongoing. But the improvements in the racial climate that have already transpired are a welcome sight. This was a course, after all, that wasn't integrated until more than 30 years after its opening. When black citizens demanded the right to golf in the late 50s, City Council's response was to sell the course rather than allow them playing privileges. Deed restrictions precluded the sale, and a court saga of more than two-year's duration ensued, before blacks were officially welcomed in 1961. Forty-five years after that watershed moment, as evidenced by the casual, golf-generated friendship between Trevor the slacker and Prince the stickler, the cultural climate has improved appreciably.

Forty-five years after that watershed moment, as evidenced by the casual, golf-generated friendship between Trevor the slacker and Prince the stickler, the cultural climate has improved appreciably.

One gorgeous spring afternoon, Head Professional Jeff Yost was walking to his booming drive on the picturesque 15th. Before sizing up his approach shot to the reachable par 5, he paused to take in the view of the marina in the middle distance. He had been brought onboard in the spring of 2005 to help right the ship, and was encouraged by the prospect of the future. "Significant changes have been made, and will continue to be made going forward to insure more consistent conditions and a better overall playing experience. We want to be one of the premiere public-access facilities in the area. Right now, this is just a place to play some golf," explains Yost in his typical earnest fashion. "But we want to turn it into a golf course."

Under his industrious, attentive stewardship and inclusive philosophy, influenced by the no-nonsense jurisdiction of his boss, Herb Whetsell, they just might make it happen.

Dunes West

Number 18, Par 4

A cliché it may be, but like many stereotypical comments of this nature, there's often an underlying nugget of truth. You can tell a lot about a golf course by the condition of its range.

Dunes West, which became affiliated with Affiniti Golf Management in 2005, has one of the finest practice facilities in the region. It goes beyond gleaming range balls, because that's often a matter of timing. Many courses either replace their balls or get them industrially cleaned a couple of times a year, and if you show up shortly thereafter, it reflects positively on the facility. But here it's also the quality of the turf - smooth, uniform, thick and unmarred. There are no ankle-breaking divots to contend with, there's no "scorched earth" policy in place. A visiting golfer's first impression is of this pristine warm-up area, which precedes a golf experience that's comfortable, straightforward and of equally high quality.

A visit to Dunes West in the northern reaches of Mt. Pleasant affords a certain symmetry. It's a larger-than-average golf property, set upon 200 acres, festooned with 200-year-old live oaks which were mere saplings when the property was known as Lexington Plantation almost 200 years ago.

There are no ankle-breaking divots to contend with, there's no "scorched earth" policy in place.

The plantation changed hands often over the years, and when the uber-wealthy, lyrically named Henrietta Hartford purchased it in 1930, she implemented some grand plans. A 32-room mansion with imported European furniture was the centerpiece. The Olmstead firm, originally founded by Frederick Law Olmstead, the famed superintendent and chief visionary of Manhattan's Central Park, was involved with the entire land plan. It included stables, gardens, tennis courts, servants and guests quarters, a saltwater swimming pool and a nine-hole golf course.

Nowadays there's no such grandiosity on display, though the clubhouse is darkly attractive in an imposing manner. But the housing surrounding the golf course, much like the condition of the turf grass throughout, is consistent. The setbacks are generous, the neighborhood homes are stately and attractive, but never showy. The development mirrors the playing fields - simple, clear-cut and attractive.

"When I came here to build, there was little information about the course that had been constructed in the 1930's and then abandoned," explains golf-course designer Art Hills. "It's where I became familiar with the word 'palimpsest' for the first time," recalls the architect of record. "It's writing material, like a parchment or tablet, used again after earlier writing has been erased," says a man who might well become a lexicographer should he ever leave golf design.

Hills' palimpsest on the property, stretching almost 6,900 yards from the farthest reaches, included a good deal of containment mounding on the fairway periphery. The multi-purpose mounding not only will help to bounce an errant ball back towards the middle and away from the omnipresent backyards, but also serves to block the cart path view somewhat, making the round a bit more pastoral in nature.

Fairways are wide, but there's a bit more anxiousness on the approach shots. The greens are mostly petite, and often surrounded by mounding and swales. They expand in size later in the round, but hit a front-side green in regulation and there'll be a legitimate birdie putt in the offing.

Fairways are wide, but there's a bit more anxiousness on the approach shots.

Dick Horne is a well-known Charleston golfer, a decorated amateur and multiple club champion. He was also one of the first people to build a home in Dunes West and has high praise for the golf course he sees everyday out his windows. "Even when the course is wet, the greens are almost always good. Arthur Hills built them right. And from the back tees, it's plenty of golf course. The 14th, for example, is 470 yards long, a par 4 that often plays into the prevailing breeze."

Routed on a north-to-south axis, the course is longish and narrow. It's constricted on the opening nine by wetlands and Wagner Creek to the west, and brushes up close to Toomer Creek near the fifth green and sixth tee. The routing consists of a pair of clockwise loops. The outward nine is a tight circle on the northern end, the inward half more of an oblong expedition with significant cart journeys required between green and tee.

Wagner Creek and a wide expanse of marshland that surrounds it make for a pretty backdrop.

The first pair of par 5's are among the more interesting holes on the front side. Both are reachable in two for a long hitter, as even from the black markers they are a smidge under 500 yards in length. But both are serious doglegs with water clearly in play. A bold corner-cutter will leave a legitimate chance to reach the green, while those of us who play station-to-station can survive with three no-better-than-average efforts.

The ninth is the prettiest hole on the property, a memorable par 4 of 370 yards. It's a slight dogleg right bisected by a narrow creek fronting one of the larger greens on the course. Before turning to the clubhouse, a player is rewarded with a wonderful vista. Wagner Creek and a wide expanse of marshland that surrounds it make for a pretty backdrop.

This 1991 creation is very playable and user friendly, with five sets of tees. The general consensus of the daily-fee customers and members is that the course is midline between pushover and punisher. There are very few at-the-turn golf ball purchases, and the post-round grumbling is almost always self-directed. There's little venom aimed at hidden hazards, encroaching tree lines or tricked-up features because they simply don't exist. It doesn't take six hours to play. And barring any unpleasant tangling with the occasional water hazard or wetland, it shouldn't take more than six golf balls to get around.

The final hole has a unique feature. This 420-yard straightaway par 4 (more than 450 yards from the tips) actually has two greens, separated by some 80 yards. The one that's almost always in use requires the longer, straighter approach. The shorter version is slightly offline to the left, nestled amid some marsh grasses. The reason they don't use "little brother" other than as an occasional novelty act is because management feels the dual yardages on sprinkler heads would be confusing, and perhaps bog down play as groups head for the clubhouse. Balderdash. In this opinion, the alternate green should be in use on a regular basis, and lend just a wee bit of pizzazz to a course that could certainly use a bit more.

Early on, the management team wanted to use some of the land adjacent to picturesque Wagner Creek as premium building lots. But the egalitarian architect, soon to fashion a useful, no-nonsense routing, persuaded them to route golf holes there instead. "I thought that those wonderful views shouldn't be the province of a few lucky property owners alone. It seemed to me that the golfers and the folks in the clubhouse should enjoy them also." And eventually, the ninth, 18th and formidable clubhouse were built just east of the scenic creek property. "We could've

made it harder, certainly," continues Hills. "But our mission was to create a user-friendly golf course that both area residents and visiting golfers could enjoy."

A workingman's architect if there ever was one, Hills remembers an anecdote from his time spent constructing Dunes West. "A guy comes up to me, a native Charlestonian, who informed me that many of the wealthy, 'old money' names in town don't actually work," recalls the 40-year veteran of the course-building trade. "In fact, he said that many of them are disdainful of those who do work for a living," says Hills, with a shake of his head. Luckily, Hills' work ethic is firmly in place, and he built a course that all golfers, be they dilettantes, 9-to-5ers, retirees or tourists can enjoy. It's a nice piece of work in its own right.

Number 17, Par 3

Of all the profile subjects envisioned for this book, I figured the hardest guy to track down would be Darius Rucker, lead singer of the rock band Hootie and the Blowfish. Virtually everyone else in the text lives and works full-time in the Charleston area, while Rucker could be jet-setting around the globe at any time. He and the boys might be the wedding band at Tiger Woods' all-star, super-secret nuptials in the Caribbean, or perhaps he's fronting the quartet in concert somewhere in Europe or South America, who knows? So imagine the shock while standing around minding my own business on a crystal-clear November morning in beautiful downtown Awendaw. Out of the blue, a well-tailored gent of medium height and build walks off the driving range, comes up to me without prompting or introduction, sticks out his hand and says, "Hi, I'm Darius Rucker." Once in a great while the mountain really does come to Mohammed.

Rucker can really roll his stone, not to mention chip it, pitch it and drive it a mile.

The Hootie honcho is a bona fide rock star, albeit not of iconic status like Mick Jagger. But unlike the emaciated Englishman, Rucker can really roll his stone, not to mention chip it, pitch it and drive it a mile. The operative word is quick. His wit is quick and so is his golf swing, he talks fast, plays fast and laughs easily with little provocation. Why shouldn't he? Life has been exceptionally good over the last decade or so, particularly compared to his childhood circumstances. The second youngest of six kids, Rucker was raised in a single-parent home by his

mom, Carolyn, a nurse. "I loved my childhood, it was a blast." he says. "I didn't realize how bad things were, how tight things were for us financially until I got much older."

Golf has been a learned skill, but "singing was like breathing to me growing up. My mom could sing, a couple of my sisters thought they could sing," he adds wryly. "Singing was always around my house. The guitar came later, out of necessity. When we started the band, I taught myself because we didn't want to hire anybody else." It's instructive to note that the multi-platinum selling Hootie and the Blowfish is the only band Rucker's ever been associated with. He and Mark Bryan, Dean Felber, and Jim Sonefeld have been making music together for some 20 years.

Rucker plays golf like most of us - erratically. He can powder the ball off the tee, but hits the odd sketchy iron. He'll knock down a drive and then come right back and knock down a couple of flagsticks in succession with some dead-on approaches. Nowhere else within this text will there be a specific mention of my own mostly mediocre golf game. But the 88 blows it took me to negotiate a windless, and therefore defenseless, Bulls Bay was particularly bereft, even by my middling standards. It was a second-rate score that felt more like a 98, considering the benign conditions, but still worth noting. Because certain scores lend themselves to catchy nicknames. "Hockey Sticks" is slang for 77, and my total of "Piano Keys" was somehow pathetically appropriate, considering I was in the company of Charleston's most famous homegrown rock-and-roller.

My personal performance on the day in question would've put an espresso-fueled insomniac into a slow doze - 16 unconverted par putts of varying lengths, which amounted to 16 bogeys and two sorry pars. My partner was more interesting to watch. Most every hole was an adventure with his birdies and double bogeys. He hit some feathery chip shots using his accumulation of local knowledge to play the ball off the slopes and swales on the massively tilting Bulls Bay greens and feed it back towards the hole. We each missed half a dozen simple putts, his mostly for birdie, and he ended up ahead by those self-same six shots on the scorecard.

Rucker is 40ish, and has been enamored of the game for more than 25 years. He learned to play on the Charleston Air Force Base course, the first time tagging along with his best friend, who was playing with his dad. "I can still remember some of the shots I hit that first day," says the rock star, who grew up without the steadying influence of a father. "I loved it right away, but the only time I could play was with them. Later that year my friend's dad gave me my first set of clubs, and I began to play whenever I could."

The West Ashley native now plays much of his golf solo, early in the day. It's not like he's lacking for friends, his Palm Pilot would be worth a fortune to a tabloid.

The West Ashley native now plays much of his golf solo, early in the day. It's not like he's lacking for friends, his Palm Pilot would be worth a fortune to a tabloid. "It can be hard to get a game early on a weekday, which is when I like to come out and play," he says. "The guys in the band like the game also, but not as much, as often or as early as I do!"

"Just like his band mates, Darius likes to have fun and knows how to enjoy a good wager," says Terry Florence, the director of golf at Bulls Bay. "We don't see as much of them as we'd like, because they are so often on the road. Darius is generous with his time, but he's a private guy, and we respect that. There's absolutely no "rock star" attitude going on. He's a well-grounded individual, a down-to-earth guy and a family man."

Rucker the Rocker has come a long way from the kid at the Air Force course or his college stomping grounds in Columbia. His University of South Carolina band mates and other golf buddies frequented a ten-dollar goat track called LinRick, which the boys called LinRock because of the stony

grounds. Back then it was all about the beer. When the band exploded into the nation's consciousness in the 90's, golf was, believe it or not, still part of the stimulus package.

"I say to people, think of everything you've ever thought about the rock-and-roll lifestyle. Now multiply that by ten. That's what things were like for us," he explains. Rucker still played golf during that heady mid- 90's rocket ride to stardom, although a morning hangover was often as much of an obstacle as the bunkering, water hazards and forests on the course of the day. "It's one of the great things about our lives. We can still call up most any course that's not super private and they'll usually invite us out to play."

"I say to people, think of everything you've ever thought about the rock-and-roll lifestyle. Now multiply that by ten. That's what things were like for us ..."

One of the main reasons he plays early in the day is to get back home to his wife Beth and three young children, Daniela, Carolyn and Darius John. But he does find time to play serious golf at serious tracks. Besides Bulls Bay, he belongs to nearby Dunes West, the posh Kiawah Island Club and the University Club in Columbia. "I love the competition of the game, even though I don't win a lot," he says, jovially. "I love to be outside, which isn't something I get to do all the time." Although he played the major sports growing up, he's not a particularly big man, and as he started to drift away from football, basketball and baseball, golf became his sport of choice. "Now it's really my only hobby. If I had a month off with nothing to do, I'd probably come out and play at least 20 times," he offers, knowing full well that an unbroken chunk of time like the one described isn't in the offing anytime soon.

The band occasionally combines rock-and-roll business with golf pleasure, and has played intermittently on tours in Scotland, Australia and New Zealand. With a hectic concert schedule, they've never managed to do more than borrow some rentals and amble about the local courses in the nearest town. It's suggested that they might want to plan an overseas tour with enough downtime built in to allow visits to the great venues of the United Kingdom and the nether reaches of the Southern Hemisphere.

"That would be too perfect," offers Rucker with a grin, a far-off look coming into his eyes.

Not too many bands that sell 20 million-plus copies of their debut album end up back on the wedding circuit, but the Blowfish boys made an exception when Tiger came a calling. "We first met back when we were still playing club dates in Michigan years ago. He was still in his teens. We've been friends ever since. It was cool to be invited to the wedding, and cool to be asked to play." Tiger is the most famous golfer on the planet, but certainly not the only megastar that Rucker is friends with, in and out of soft spikes. Davis Love III and John Daly are good friends, as are actor Joe Pesci, quarterback Dan Marino, ESPN anchor Dan Patrick and dozens upon dozens of other "A"-list celebrities. Not hard to understand, when you play annually in marquee PGA Tour celebrity events like the Bob Hope Chrysler Classic and the AT&T National Pro-Am at Pebble Beach.

Not too many bands that sell 20 million-plus copies of their debut album end up back on the wedding circuit ...

These soirees are all well and good, but Rucker prefers to see his high-profile friends back in South Carolina, at Hootie's very own hootenanny, called the "Monday after the Masters" event, which they've been hosting for more than a dozen years. The Hootie gang inveigles dozens of their musical colleagues, actors, athletes and PGA pros to participate in this immensely popular Celebrity Pro-Am. Because of their enthusiastic support and sponsorship, more than $3 million has been raised for the Hootie and the Blowfish Foundation, a charitable entity that benefits a wide range of educational projects, junior-golf programs and various needy entities in the South Carolina school system. "We were tired of seeing our state with such a low national ranking in education, so we decided to do something about it," says the Middleton High School grad.

Rucker and the band are branching further in this direction, now involving themselves with higher education. The year 2005 will mark the debut of The Hootie, a brand-new collegiate golf tournament. The University of South Carolina, Clemson and the College of Charleston golf squads will co-host this gathering of some of the nation's finest teams. With a dramatic venue like Bulls Bay as the backdrop and post-round entertainment provided by the band, the event will undoubtedly be an instant success and quickly grow in popularity.

The devotion to native soil is still very much in evidence, though there has been so much road time in the last 20-odd years. "I lived in New York for awhile, but eventually decided that Charleston is where I'm supposed to be," he offers. "It's funny, I used to make fun of my sisters for coming back home to live. It sounds corny, but this is home. There are other factors also. You can tell that golf is very important to me, and the golf scene is great. I love the weather. The people are the nicest people in the world. The main reason is the fact I grew up here, my whole family is here, brothers, sisters, cousins. When I step off a plane at the airport I know I'm home."

Of course, no place is perfect, Charleston very much included. Racism was an almost everyday occurrence when Rucker was coming up in the early 70's. "It's just the way it was back then, be it kids in school, coaches. There were always casual comments made that were inappropriate and bigoted." Dozens of years and millions of dollars later, things have changed. But not thoroughly. "It still happens, but not as much. This city and the South in general have come a long way, but things could always improve." As an example, the man who revels in the playing invites he's received to some of the world's finest courses mentions an old-line local club on which he's never set foot. "Never been invited, and to be honest, until they have a black member I wouldn't go over there if I was," he says.

"I lived in New York for awhile, but eventually decided that Charleston is where I'm supposed to be," he offers. "It's funny, I used to make fun of my sisters for coming back home to live. It sounds corny, but this is home."

Hootie and the Blowfish have been deemed passé by certain music critics and pundits, who've disdained them as a one-album wonder. That first disc was a bona fide phenomenon, one of the top-15 sellers in history. The total sales of several follow-up albums in the years since that dominating debut haven't added up to the numbers they achieved the first time out. But so what? It's instructive to compare Rucker to his friend Tiger, with whom he's had a friendship since well before they each hit it big. Golf fans will recall that Woods won his first Masters as a professional in 1997 by an astounding 12 strokes, and set dozens of all-time records in doing so. Now pretend for a moment that Tiger didn't win the 2000 U.S. Open three years later by 15 shots at Pebble Beach, and instead won the event by just a couple of strokes. If he never won another Major in the same dominating fashion as he did the first time out, does it somehow diminish the original accomplishment? Of course not.

"No, we'll never replicate the success we had with our debut album 'Cracked Rear View,'" admits Rucker as we head for the clubhouse, belying the fact that both his legacy and bank account are secure in perpetuity regardless. "We were in the right place at the right time, just as the era of 'grunge' rock was ending." He chuckles one more time and says, "We never expected it to happen the first time. How can we ever expect it to happen again?"

The Links at Stono Ferry

Number 13, Par 4

Question: How many Charlestonians does it take to change a light bulb?

Answer: Seven. One to change it, and half a dozen more to say they preferred things the way they were.

This silly joke underscores the "leave it alone" mentality that serves as an undercurrent throughout much of the city. But not even the most hidebound golf-loving traditionalist could've objected to the changes and drastic improvements made at the Links at Stono Ferry in recent times. The impressive 1989 Ron Garl design located some 20 minutes south of downtown has enjoyed a wonderful resurgence in the last few years. The setting has never been in question, just the commitment to quality.

"I was initially attracted to the natural variety that occurs on this land parcel," says the architect. "It's the frontage on the river, the lakes that dot the property, the wonderful size and quality of the oaks and pines. I was shocked to see trees of that stature growing in such proximity to the salt water." Stono Ferry's location in the town of Hollywood is somehow apt, as after an extended dark period, the course is once again a rising star in Charleston's public golf galaxy.

... the course is once again a rising star in Charleston's public golf galaxy.

If there's a single reason for the renaissance of the property it's because Pat Barber thought his neighborhood golf course was something of an eyesore. The 40-something businessman heard the course was available for purchase back in 2002, and decided to get into the golf business.

"I've lived near the property for more than 10 years and always loved the course," explains the soft-spoken Barber. "Every time I played someone would comment how the course had such beautiful holes and wonderful trees and spectacular scenery. But the maintenance wasn't up to speed, and the potential of the property was so far above what was being offered, mostly because previous ownership groups were more concerned with taking money out of the course as opposed to putting it back in. I decided we could really have something special here if things were done right, so I bought it myself."

Key members of the management team hired by the previous ownership group American Golf Corporation have remained onboard with Barber. Those whose tenure has straddled each regime cite the ease and efficiency of dealing with an accessible and hands-on owner. This is in contrast to the previous standard, which meant navigating through hierarchical management levels at a corporation with 300 separate golf properties.

Stono Ferry was named the 2003/2004 Charleston Area Golf Course of the Year.

This hands-on approach has yielded some impressive results. Membership has grown from about 60 to more than 225, and shortly after Barber's purchase, Stono Ferry was named the 2003/2004 Charleston Area Golf Course of the Year. New Champion Bermuda-grass greens have replaced its disease-prone predecessor. There have been major improvements made to the course infrastructure, a new island green has been installed to make the par-4 finisher one to remember, and there has been a substantial increase in maintenance staff, equipment and attention. Stono Ferry is now in very nice condition, and management is absolutely committed to systematically improving the quality of the golf experience even further. Golfers who've been in absentia in recent years will be shocked to see what has transpired in the interim.

This is a serpentine, 6,700-yard routing, quite short by modern standards. Though the outward nine represents half of the golf course and slightly more than

half of the total yardage, the absolute lion's share of the attraction and memorability of this venue is on the inward journey. There are several nice holes on the opening nine, and a pastoral setting that actually includes some horses grazing adjacent to a fairway or two. "My goal is to design courses that sit softly on the land, that aren't overly intrusive with contrived features, sharp angles or heavy-handed bunkering," explains Garl. "There's no reason to over-manufacture hazards on a course that offers them naturally." But if the front is only fine, with a lower case "f," then the back nine, by contrast, is what will make you want to return.

First off, several of the holes are target oriented, with forced carries from the tee over water and wetlands that weren't part of the landscape previously. Second, holes 12 through 14 abut the Stono River, and offer some of the most wonderful views of any golf course in greater Charleston.

The 12th is a lovely par 4 leading towards the water. It's only 360 yards from the back tee, but a wetland pinching the landing area provides some trepidation. The next is tinier still, a par 4 straining to crack the 350-yard barrier, but with another tricky tee shot and dazzling waterside scenery. The 14th is a medium-length par 3 with an angled tee box practically perched in the river. "The water holes provide the 'wow' factor for most people, but I am just as impressed with the quality and consistency of the tree canopies," says Ron Garl.

The 12th is a lovely par 4 leading towards the water. It's only 360 yards from the back tee, but a wetland pinching the landing area provides some trepidation.

Lastly and most uniquely, this same stretch of holes was a Revolutionary War battleground, and there are monuments posted intermittently that provide some of the details of this 1779 conflict that left some 300 soldiers mortally wounded, including Andrew Jackson's older brother. (See what I mean about the details?) A full 210 years before golf balls were fired about the property, American patriots and British Army forces fired upon each other in a bloody conflict eventually won by the Brits. Some 70 years after the battle, the Charleston and Savannah Railroad was routed through this same stretch of property. This intercity lifeline between the kindred cities remained active until the mid-60's, falling into disuse a couple of decades before the golf course was born. Charleston will always be more about history than golf, and no area golf venue provides such an up-close, "you are there" history lesson on the playing field itself.

These three successive waterside beauties comprise less than 13 percent of the total course yardage, so to make a whole-hearted recommendation requires more beef than just this tantalizing trio. As players move away from the water and turn for home, they are confronted with some staunch challenges. The 15th is a 525-yard dogleg par 5, but big hitters can skirt the corner and get home in two.

The next is a lengthy dogleg par 4, the penultimate hole another strapping par 5, and the last, as mentioned earlier, a 340-yard cutie with a devilish island green. Stono may be a bit sleepy from the get-go, but rest assured you'll be at full attention coming down the homestretch.

... no area golf venue provides such an up-close, "you are there" history lesson on the playing field itself.

The growing reputation of the course is due to a combination of factors. The variety, scenery and improving course quality are all important, and so is proximity. This is the nearest public-access venue to Kiawah Island, and though Stono is not promoted as a "value" course, the simple fact is that the greens fees here are but a fraction of the resort offerings down Kiawah or Seabrook way. So they've managed to siphon some players from the posh resorts, who must be thrilled to get a fistful of bills back in change when they push a Ben Franklin across the pro shop counter. In a cutthroat golf climate where operators are fighting to keep their share of a shrinking pie, where reduced greens fees and time-of-day discounts have become the watchword, Stono's annual rounds have remained steady and course revenue has increased markedly. They are surely doing something right. "Golf courses are organisms that are continually evolving, and it's gratifying to now have an owner in place that's intent on bringing the course up to the highest standard possible," concludes Garl.

Renowned detective novelist Raymond Chandler once exclaimed, "If my books had been any worse, I should not have been invited to Hollywood, and if they had been any better, I should not have come." He was, of course, referring to California's city of dreams. I might've answered the same way previously, though my rural Hollywood is almost 2,500 miles east of his. But that was before taking a couple of tours of the new-look Links at Stono Ferry. I'm glad to have been invited, and equally glad to have come. Discriminating golfers who make the same journey will surely feel the same way.

"If my books had been any worse, I should not have been invited to Hollywood, and if they had been any better, I should not have come."

ESSAY: MY FAVORITE COURSE

Golf course architect Geoffrey Cornish's legacy will likely always evoke the word quantity rather than quality. Having enjoyed life into his 90s, the Canadian native created or refurbished close to 250 courses over the years, working mostly in New England. A couple of his layouts have gained some prominence, most notably The International in central Massachusetts and Stratton Mountain in southern Vermont. But as a general rule, Cornish designs are modestly budgeted, efficiently produced and offer little flair.

Crestview is a comfortable and comforting course, though, not unlike an old pair of jeans or a well-washed sweatshirt.

Many of my seminal golf moments occurred on a track you might call quintessential Cornish, Crestview Country Club, laid upon the mostly flat farmland in the western Massachusetts town of Agawam. The View, as it's known to some, is a well-conditioned and well-balanced par 72, with a pair of one-shot and three-shot holes on both the outward and inward nines. It's inaccurate to call it my "favorite" course; anyone who's been fortunate enough to trod the fairways of Pine Valley and Portmarnock, Pebble Beach and Pinehurst No. 2 would be hard-pressed to name another as superior. Crestview is a comfortable and comforting course, though, not unlike an old pair of jeans or a well-washed sweatshirt. It might be lacking in style, but it's solid, sensible and straightforward.

I'm a thousand miles from The View these days, but I've marched the property at least that many times over the years, and could still do so blindfolded. It was the site of many important firsts for me. For starters, it was the site of my first kiss and my first par, taking place concurrently one preteen summer. I don't recall much about the former, other than it took place behind the tennis backboard, and before commencing included a warning that there would be "no wandering hands." The par I still remember. It came on the tough opening hole, a par-4 dogleg right with a narrow fairway. I boomed a drive off the elevated tee, crushed a fairway wood, wedged on from somewhere well short of the green and made the putt. I

assume my kissing technique has improved over these last 30-odd years, but I'm ashamed to admit I still make a disproportionate number of pars in much the same fashion.

Crestview afforded me my first "golf gang," served as a training ground for gambling, and was also the site of my first tournament triumph, albeit in a lowly member-guest. It was there I first broke 90, broke 80, and then broke my own spirit when I couldn't break par. One supernatural day, I birdied the benign 17th and lurched unsteadily to the final tee box at a heart-hammering 1 under. I let out a roar of triumph after yet another drive found the center stripe, avoiding pitfalls both right and left. I had a perfect lie, a 7-iron approach to the elevated green, and a song in my heart, but my elation quickly gave way to abomination. Five minutes and five shots later, I tapped in numbly for a double-bogey 6, and a then personal-best 73. The beer was strangely flat in the 19th hole, matching my mood perfectly. I knew deep down I had let a golden opportunity slip away, and my intuition proved correct. It's been well over 10 years since that fateful day, and I've yet to better par.

Crestview afforded me my first "golf gang," served as a training ground for gambling, and was also the site of my first tournament triumph, albeit in a lowly member-guest.

These days there's no shortage of dedicated golfers at The View, but for a long time the membership was less enthusiastic. A nearby Donald Ross gem provides contrast. The Orchards is a wonderful track near Mount Holyoke College in South Hadley, and played host to the 2004 U.S. Women's Open. The Orchards was always known as a real golf club, with an avid and skilled membership. Their modest clubhouse and dining area served as an indication that the facility was no-frills, and the game was the thing. Crestview, featuring a gaudy and god-awful clubhouse, a monument to 50's kitsch, was known in the area as a restaurant that happened to be surrounded by a golf course.

When I was a kid, the Kringle family ran the golf operation. Frank Kringle was a hell of a stick, a good teacher and wonderful man. His wife, Louise, ran the shop, and their son, Frannie, was the assistant pro. Frank held onto his skills for eons. Once he was old enough, he was shooting his age as easily as most people shoot their mouths off, albeit less regularly. They're all gone now; ma and pa deceased, and Frannie, who eventually filled his father's position but never his shoes, onto other things.

The View was the first place I putted with my daughter, the last place I golfed with my dad ...

The View was the first place I putted with my daughter, the last place I golfed with my dad, and the site of my first, and to this point only, ace. I caromed a 6- iron off the bank on the left side of the picturesque 11th, and reached down to pick up my tee when I saw the ball was rebounding towards the putting surface. I didn't believe the deed was done till I saw the ball in the hole, owing to my poker-faced companion. There was no disbelief in his tone, or joy, exultation or excitement. He just said flatly, "It's in the hole," the way someone would say, "You're away" or "I'm playing a Strata." For a long while I couldn't figure out why, and then the answer came to me. Jealousy is an ugly trait. My miracle shot occurred late on a weekday afternoon near Halloween, and afterward I stood in the pro shop for almost an hour, sounding like a desperate single in the throes of Happy Hour. I kept repeating "Can I buy you a drink?" to the smattering of folks wandering through the shop, but there were no takers. I don't recall where my aggrieved witness disappeared to, but I guess he was expected elsewhere.

... it's just a slight exaggeration to suggest that there are only two golf seasons: lift, clean and place, and August.

By and large, The View is a pretty place. It blooms nicely in the spring, and goes ablaze in autumn. Drainage has always been a serious concern, though. The course retains water like a camel, and it's just a slight exaggeration to suggest that there are only two golf seasons: lift, clean and place, and August.

A longtime member and good pal of mine always reminds me that Crestview is "a good everyday course." He's right, but owing to its status as the former home of the Friendly's Classic, a now-defunct LPGA tour stop that was sponsored by the New England-based restaurant chain, perhaps an ice cream analogy is more appropriate. Rating, reviewing and writing about golf courses affords me the opportunity to set foot on some of the finest greensward in the land. Living in coastal Georgia, I spend most of my time on the lush courses of the Lowcountry, and the crown jewels of Hilton Head, Beaufort, Sea Island, Savannah and of course greater Charleston in particular are as sweet and delightful as cinnamon swirl. I work in the intermountain West as well, and the combination of thin mountain air, precipitous drops and dizzying views combine for an exhilarating golf experience full of surprises, like eating rocky road. I often golf my way through eastern Massachusetts in summer, and the timeless courses, storied venues and historic clubhouses peopled with Boston Brahmins offer a rich and traditional experience, like a classic banana split. But I also enjoy the view from The View, and when I happen by the area, it's always a pleasure to tee it up with my old fellows. Sometimes, you get a craving for vanilla.

Patriots Point

MOUNT PLEASANT, SOUTH CAROLINA

Number 17, Par 3

Jonathan Ray looks professorial, with his tweedy suit, bowtie and spectacles. His family came to Charleston in the early 1700's, which partially accounts for his wealth of local knowledge. He's also quite friendly and approachable, which makes him perfect for his job as club concierge at one of the city's finest hotels, Charleston Place.

"Patriots Point is not only the No. 1 tourist attraction in Charleston, but in all of South Carolina," explains Ray, describing the aircraft carrier Yorktown stationed in Charleston Harbor. "Frankly, I personally don't understand the appeal. It has all the ambience of a floating prison." Ray acknowledges that much of the attraction has to do with our collective respect and admiration for the World War II

"Greatest Generation," and the resurgence of patriotism seen in the country in the last several years. Besides the massive carrier, there's a destroyer, Coast Guard cutter and submarine on site, along with the Congressional Medal of Honor museum. But the concierge shrugs and then sniffs, "There's really not that much going on."

The same can be said for the Links at Patriots Point. This is another supposed attraction of the site, located just east of the downtown peninsula on the western end of Mt. Pleasant. It's no "floating prison," as the wry Mr. Ray might remark, but by the same token it's no great charmer. Yes, there are some excellent sweeping water views as a player turns for home. But too much of this mostly cookie-cutter course is

Patriots Point, Charleston in background.

marred by intrusions like radio towers and thoroughfares, views of budget hotel chains and strip centers. A pastoral walk in the park it's not.

It's a surprisingly well-conditioned course, considering Patriots Point sees more than 40,000 rounds annually.

Willard Byrd is the architect of record on this 6,900-yard track, which debuted in 1981. There have been a number of fingers in the pie in the succeeding 25 or so years, including those of course designer Bob Spence, who was in the middle of a $5 million renovation in 1997.

It's a surprisingly well-conditioned course, considering Patriots Point sees more than 40,000 rounds annually. Although the logical conclusion drawn is that tourists provide the bulk of the course revenue after visiting the adjacent military attractions, the fact is that 60 percent of the play is generated by locals. This is due in part to the moderating temperatures on the point of land where the course is located. Rumor has it that Patriots Point is a full 10 degrees cooler in summertime than most of greater Charleston.

What isn't as cool is the less-than-inspired layout. Regardless of the fact that a player is less likely to break a sweat at Patriots Point than elsewhere in town, it's quite obvious that Mr. Byrd didn't exactly break a sweat himself while laying out the course.

Byrd passed away late in 2004 at the age of 85, but was quoted quite memorably 15 years earlier. "Golf course architecture is just fancy farming," he said. No disrespect intended, because he produced some fine courses in the Southeast during his long career. But there's nothing too fancy about Patriots Point.

The bunkers are mostly flattish saucers of sand. The greens have a bit of movement to them, but are pretty basic overall. The course has a back-and-forth rhythm with little imagination. Playing corridors are wide and predominantly runway straight. The new Ravenel Bridge dominates the landscape. It's an impressive sight in the middle distance, with the sleek cables and diamond-shaped towers almost 600 feet high. Too bad that midway through the outward nine the bridge views give way to close-ups of less inspiring man-made creations, as the intrusions of traffic and commerce sully the experience just a bit.

The course plays differently from the white markers

to the blues, and it goes beyond the excess 500 yards (6,900 yards with a 129 slope from the outer limits, just a shade below 6,400 yards and sloped at 123 in the truncated version). Besides the additional mileage, the angles off the tee are different, as are the perspectives to the fairway.

Byrd passed away late in 2004 at the age of 85, but was quoted quite memorably 15 years earlier. "Golf course architecture is just fancy farming," he said.

Patriots Point receives an overall passing grade, though, because it concludes with a degree of panache missing through the first two-thirds of the routing. The 13th is an interesting pond-fronted par 5, where only a booming drive will allow contemplation of getting home in two. The next is a strong par 3 aimed directly at the harbor, though the bend of the landscape camouflages any water view. The last few holes offer a couple of subtle angles to the green on shorter par 4's, along with a petite par-3 17th, featuring a poor man's island green. Standing on the penultimate green affords a lovely view across the water, the downtown spires jutting gracefully into the sky. It's only 10 holes past the cacophonous traffic of the strip centers, but from this vantage point it seems more like 10 miles.

This course review might well lose its relevancy in the coming years, and the preceding opinion could be rendered moot. Patriots Point is potentially slated for a total redo in the future, or so rumor has it. The schedule isn't calling for a nip and tuck, but the whole Joan Rivers treatment. Some marquee architect (Jack Nicklaus has been the most prevalent name bandied about) might be coming to town and starting over from scratch. With apologies to the folks at the Indianapolis 500, the most positive thing one can say is, "Gentlemen, start your bulldozers."

Patriots Point is pleasant enough in the final analysis, as the final flurry of holes make what has been a pedestrian experience to that point somewhat memorable. But in a culinary capital such as Charleston, it's a bit like having dinner at a franchise joint like Chili's or Applebee's. The food is passable and there'll be no surprises, you've seen it all before. But similar to the area's expanding golf scene, there are myriad restaurant choices far more interesting and worthwhile.

River Towne

Number 8 tee box, Number 7 green

Here's a little secret about Charleston's public golf offerings: Most are a little long in the tooth. If they're not 15 years old, then they're closer to 30. Not so in the private sector, where shiny new venues like Bulls Bay, Briar's Creek and Daniel Island are all of this century. But the pay-as-you-play crowd is stuck mostly with hand-me-downs from a previous era. The operative word being "mostly."

RiverTowne Country Club in Mount Pleasant, the first Arnold Palmer Signature Course in greater Charleston, is a refreshing change. This 2002 creation offers a baker's dozen worth of holes featuring views of the Wando River and Horlbeck Creek, and is a well-kept, ultra-challenging adventure. With all the water come plenty of wetlands, lurking semi-hid-den on the periphery of many a fairway. Palmer and company have built some sizeable rolling shoulders on the periphery of the short grass. This mounding provides some attractive definition and will help contain, or at least slow down, subtly offline shots headed for oblivion.

He may be The King, but golf cognoscenti have been reluctant to anoint Arnold Palmer as architectural royalty.

"Country Club for a Day" is an expression that has thankfully fallen by the wayside in describing public or resort golf offerings, but RiverTowne is as close as it gets, certainly north of the city, anyway.

He may be The King, but golf cognoscenti have been reluctant to anoint Arnold Palmer as architectural royalty. This vagabond golfer has played plenty of rounds on Palmer tracks that were fair to middling, and only a couple on venues that were truly a cut above. Why has the designer failed to secure the architectural reputation of a Nicklaus, Weiskopf or Crenshaw? There are several theories. Some say the design team backing him is only average, and his tendency to take on too much work at once dilutes the finished product. Another reason given is he's had limited access to premiere land parcels, but there was plenty to work with at RiverTowne and he took full advantage of the opportunity.

Like Palmer in his prime, RiverTowne is burly, broad-shouldered and intimidating. Arnie was a swashbuckler back in the day, and his aggressiveness, occasionally his uneven play, cost him several Major championships. There's a bit of unevenness in this design also. Holes like the 540-yard, par-5 ninth are awkward, with its ultra-demanding second shot and an almost-invisible water hazard lurking greenside. The three-shot 11th is another head-scratcher, with a tree leaning over the green. The 15th is a monstrous dogleg of almost 450 yards from the gold markers (the tips are closer to 475), yet the fairway cants away from the dogleg and the end result is a tee shot that generally bounds farther away from the already distant green.

There are a number of fine holes, though, and most are framed by gorgeous marsh grasses and wetlands. But then beauty can be in the eye of the beholder. The waving vegetation is downright ugly if your golf ball isn't flying above and beyond, but instead plummeting into the reeds bracketing so many of the fairways.

Like Palmer in his prime, RiverTowne is burly, broad-shouldered and intimidating.

This golf course covers a tremendous amount of acreage. The outward loop meanders in a counterclockwise fashion, while the inward nine returns clockwise to the clubhouse. While proceeding in opposite directions, both nines are characterized by expansive fairways, abundant water hazards, lots of vegetation and numerous doglegs both gentle and severe.

RiverTowne will be an absolute bear for golfers who lose their stamina and swing as the round progresses. The penultimate markers are almost 6,700 yards in length with a 135 slope, the championship tees sloped at a sky-high 147 and almost 7,200 yards long. But in both cases, the inward journey has significantly more heft that the outward. From the gold tees (not the back-of-the-box blacks), most of the front-side par 4's are well under 400 yards, including the pip-squeak sixth that checks in at 280. The return journey is a different story, with one par 4 a hair below and another just a hair above 400, while the remaining trio are 430, 440 and close to 450 yards in length. Sage advice: Don't have a power outage as you head for the majestic clubhouse, or if so, prepare to chip and one-putt for your pars.

The opening hole offers a fairly gentle beginning, assuming you can steer the ball away from the lagoon to the right and bunkers waiting left. From the penultimate markers, this right-angle dogleg is but 355 yards. But the next is a real wakeup call, especially if you've stepped all the way back to the black markers. The championship tees require a marsh carry of some 215 yards on this bulkhead par 3. Less intrepid souls playing from one of the other four sets of markers have a much shorter shot. More importantly, the angle to the green comes from an entirely different perspective, and the daunting marsh carry existing from the tips is excised entirely. The sixth is just 310 from the tips and offers an intriguing drive-the-green opportunity. Cerebral players, especially those longer on course sense and shorter off the tee, will take the conservative route and attempt to wedge their way to birdie.

A blind tee shot on the 10th continues, actually intensifies, the theme of hidden hazards. It's not a totally straightforward golf course, with everything well out in front and visible. The ebb and flow of power versus placement subsides as the round winds towards conclusion. Finesse shots give way to pure firepower. Two of the best holes in succession are among the toughest. Nos. 12 and 13 are brawny par 4's of 430 and 405 yards respectively, the latter with a green teetering on the edge of a marsh. As mentioned earlier, the flawed 15th is a gauntlet and the final hole is the capper. This is another dogleg of 440 yards with the wind from the Wando hurting the cause, water and the ubiquitous wetlands flanking the left side all the way. It's a tough finish to a terrific test of golf.

Number 13, Par 4

Although the forward men's tees compact the course yardage to 5,800 and the ladies markers are just under 5,100, RiverTowne is no beginner's affair. Time and again, a player must stand and deliver - over water or weeds, between the woods and the marshes. It's not a "hit it, find it, hit it again" type of course.

But never have I spied an honest-to-goodness bald eagle, lording off the first tee imperiously, as was witnessed at RiverTowne.

The inherent drama tee to green makes it easy to overlook the putting surfaces themselves, but many are notable. The penultimate hole is a 175-yard, tabby-walled par 3 over an acre of cabbage, and has a magnificent hourglass green. There are two skill sets necessary here. First, one must be able to clear the hazard and find purchase on the surface. But an inaccurate iron or utility wood will leave an untenable putt, in all likelihood an impossible putt that might stretch to 100 feet or more.

It seems eight out of 10 golf course brochures tout the wide range of wildlife that calls that particular course home. I've been fortunate to see flora and fauna of all kinds in my travels, including fairway-crossing moose in both New Hampshire and Minnesota. But never have I spied an honest-to-goodness bald eagle, lording off the first tee imperiously, as was witnessed at RiverTowne. This was the majestic national symbol, the real deal, the bird you see right on your money. Speaking of which, there are plenty of golf establishments all over town to spend yours, but one of the easiest arguments to make is to spend it at RiverTowne. Save a couple of quirky holes, for those with enough game, it's right on the money as well.

Shadowmoss Plantation

Number 16, Par 3

Because of its rich, centuries-old history, Charleston possesses a hierarchical culture rarely seen in other places. A recent transplant might be impressed that his next-door neighbor's family has been in town for three generations. But that neighbor looks with envy at a co-worker whose great-great-grandfather came to Charleston in the 19th century. And to the tenth-generation Charlestonian whose ancestry included rice, cotton or indigo planters, all of them are carpetbaggers.

Similarly, the Charleston golf scene has a pecking order of its own. There are the marquee names that give the city its ultimate golf identity, be they the classic venues from yesteryear or the modern mega-resorts with massive promotional budgets. But there

are other worthwhile courses around, venues that receive scant attention by comparison. These facilities have lower profiles, lower advertising expenditures and lower greens fees. They are the type of courses that a cost-conscious traveler might visit with a different set of expectations. Shadowmoss Plantation, about 20 minutes south of downtown, is such a course. But as evidenced by its busy pro shop, convivial tavern, brisk on-course business and full parking lot, they are surely doing something right.

Head Professional J.P. Ringer describes the unique appeal of a club that has remained somewhat under the radar of the visiting golfer, but has become practically a cult favorite for Lowcountry locals. "We have a tremendously loyal clientele," he explains. "We have all sorts of regular games, daily groups, blitzes, golf gangs and the like. It's pretty much nonstop around here."

Shadowmoss is also the only course in town that offers a money-back guarantee.

Despite the presence of semi-legendary groups like the Wild Bunch, the Gators, the Over the Hill Gang and the Nooners, Shadowmoss is a course that also caters carefully to traveling golfers. Although places like Kiawah Resort and Wild Dunes will always get the lion's share of the attention, not all players are willing to pay a premium greens fee for every single round on vacation. That's why a visit to this sporty Russell Breeden design south of town, twice the host of the South Carolina Open, is something to take under careful consideration.

Shadowmoss is also the only course in town that offers a money-back guarantee. If a player isn't enjoying himself when he makes the turn, management will refund the greens fee. It almost never happens. The Champion Ultra-Dwarf greens installed in 2003 are usually in excellent shape, and the course routing through the neighborhood subdivision is pleasant enough. The front-nine par 5's and back-side par 3's are among the on-course highlights, but the true appeal of Shadowmoss goes beyond the strategic elements of the course itself. The most notable facet of the club is the loyal clientele that shows up to play in all seasons and for all reasons. The course is at its essence a character study, and to belabor the shot values and occasional architectural highlights is somewhat irrelevant. It's like writing a restaurant review of Charleston's funkiest, liveliest barbecue joint and concentrating on the quality of the flatware instead of the food. At Shadowmoss, it's the people that make the difference.

He is the grandson of a hotel magnate whose name is instantly recognizable, and has the financial wherewithal to join the ritziest courses in the county. But he loves Shadowmoss.

"The Legend" sits down post-round, sparing a few minutes before shepherding his grade school daughter to a play date. This 40-something course regular and neighborhood dweller lives directly off a back-nine fairway. He is the grandson of a hotel magnate whose name is instantly recognizable, and has the financial wherewithal to join the ritziest courses in the county. But he loves Shadowmoss.

"I've never called and made a tee time here in all the years I've been a member. There is always something happening - an outing, a tournament, a member function. I can show up and play with guys I like and never want for a game. I like the design of the course, also," continues the Legend. "The back-side par 3's are probably the most dynamic in Charleston. They are long, tough and beautiful." He speaks of the 12th, which pushes 190 from the blue markers, with gold tees that are 20 yards longer still. There are woods left, and a sizeable pond right. Slicers beware. The 16th is sweet in its own right, necessitating another daunting blow of 200 yards to find a green protected by bunkers and water.

Kyle Bibler is another club member in a unique position. He's a fine player and three-time club champion. He's also the head superintendent of the Golf Club at Briar's Creek, which is 30 minutes and tax brackets away. He's employed at an ultra-private, big-ticket Johns Island retreat where the founding member's initiation fee alone would allow daily access to Shadowmoss for some 60 years. The courses are as closely related as the Washingtons, Denzel and George.

The courses are as closely related as the Washingtons, Denzel and George.

"I love the layout here, and it goes beyond the par-3 holes, which are our signature. The par 5's are strong, several of which are reachable, and the par 4's offer a good variety of length and direction." The best of the long holes is the eighth, where the elbow of a stream imposes on the right side of the fairway, necessitating a careful tee shot. No member is more qualified to expound on the maintenance issues than this wild man of the Wild Bunch, who makes his way to the course about three days a week on average. "There are some shade issues that need to be dealt with here, and the ongoing tree trimming and removal will improve conditions going forward." Bibler pays a compliment to his fellow greenskeeper, acknowledging he puts the "super" in superintendent. "Wayne Stonaker does a phenomenal job. He does 10 times as many rounds here and works with one-third of the annual budget that I have. I truly admire the condition he maintains here," says Bibler, who has been in charge at Briar's Creek since opening day in 2000.

Doc Shoaff is another longtime member. In his casual golf togs, this mid-single-digit-handicapper bears a passing resemblance to Mr. Green Jeans of Captain Kangaroo fame, though Doc's denim is of the traditional blue variety. He looks a bit provincial with his workman's pants and bucket hat, belying the fact he was a former Marine helicopter pilot who ended up earning a dental degree. "The course demands accuracy, which is my strong suit," acknowledges the man known as "Down-the-middle-Doc." "It's only 6,700 yards from the tips, and 6,400 yards from where we normally play. If you can keep it in the fairway you'll be okay." Approach shots from the short grass mean there's a better chance to hit it close on large greens with plenty of tilt and slope. But wayward drivers will be contending with shallow bunkers, mounding, ditches and the occasional out-of-bounds stakes delineating backyard boundaries.

> *"There are a number of courses in the area that are just as convenient, that are almost as good a value," concludes Doc. "But it's really the camaraderie here. This place is like home."*

"There are a number of courses in the area that are just as convenient, that are almost as good a value," concludes Doc. "But it's really the camaraderie here. This place is like home." Though they won't know the regulars bellying up to the bar, talking trash while settling bets, visitors almost always enjoy Shadowmoss regardless. The colorful cadre of regulars makes the traveling golfer popping by for a round feel right at home as well.

Number 18, Par 4

I'm something of an expert on golf maladies, because in the course of a mostly star-crossed career, I've had 'em all. Right now I occasionally do battle with one of the most perverse entities known to man, the dreaded sideways shot. I won't utter the technical term out loud, nor will I write it, but it's a heinous affliction that begins with the letters "s" and "h". If you're thinking of the cussword and not the golf shot, that's okay too, as it's pretty much the same thing.

"That was a pretty nice up, up, up and down."

The actual yips haven't yet affected me, but I've missed dozens upon dozens of extremely short putts over the years, so maybe they have. There have been periods when I couldn't extricate my ball from the bunker, sometimes taking as many as four blows from a perfectly serviceable lie. (After holing a lengthy putt when finally freed from the sand, a wise guy once said to me, memorably, "That was a pretty nice up, up, up and down.") There were times when I hit irons consistently fat, tearing up great clods of turf which traveled half the distance of my pitifully short attempted approach shot.

"What was that? An 11-wood?"

Overcompensation inevitably occurred as well, and blading the ball became a problem. An envisioned high, soft wedge shot nestling near the flag instead morphed into a screaming, waist-high Scud missile, destined for the underbrush or lurking lateral hazard, never to be heard from again. One summer I suffered through a brief but brutal period where I was terrified of hitting an iron off a tee, and approached every short hole with unwarranted trepidation. The nadir (apex?) of this affliction occurred when I hit a small, choked-down utility wood on a 110-yard, downhill par 3. I carved it in to four feet and made the deuce, but was still mortified when the stranger I was playing with asked, "What was that? An 11-wood?"

All of these golf troubles are disheartening to say the least. But there's one that's even worse: not being able to keep the tee shot in play. I was recently cold-cocked with this reality, watching one of my good golf pals suffer through the worst driving day since Ted Kennedy was on Chappaquiddick Island.

The Phantom is a good guy, a close business associate, a decent (albeit deliberate) player, and most importantly, a steady cash supply for this needy correspondent. Phantom is unnaturally flexible, and as a result, supernaturally long off the tee. If we both catch a good drive on a reasonably long par 4, I'm thrilled to have a mid iron in my hand instead of the usual fairway wood. He, often 50 yards ahead, expects to attack with a pitching wedge. That's just the way it is. Hoop coaches say "you can't teach height," and in the same vein, I'm convinced the same holds true with length. You either have it or you don't.

... watching one of my good golf pals suffer through the worst driving day since Ted Kennedy was on Chappaquiddick Island.

In any event, on the day in question the Phantom simply could not get his driver to behave. He must've put close to 30 balls on tees instead of the requisite 18, so often was he playing a provisional. The "diving, over-spinning lefts" are an unwelcome illness on any golf course, but especially in and around Charleston, with many courses featuring homes lining the fairways and OB stakes ubiquitous, it's a particularly virulent disease. Reloading on the tee even once in a while really stinks. But having to do so hole after hole is golf misery personified, because a player is defeated from the outset. Golfers are a naïve lot, because we can't help but play the game with unfounded optimism. When a drive is in the fairway or light rough, the approach shot on or close to the green, when an errant shot is found sitting nicely in the woods with an opening through the trees, as long as the ball can be advanced in some meaningful way, a player remains hopeful about the outcome to follow. Conversely, if every wayward tee shot must be played out sideways, or even worse, is found to be off the golf course entirely, it makes for a long and depressing afternoon. Then you're stuck playing defensive golf, scrambling golf, hoping-to-salvage-bogey golf. No fun.

I felt bad for the Phantom as we parted ways in the

twilight, though there was much to feel good about. A mutual business project had debuted that very day to glowing reviews, he was peeling off twenties instead of fives or singles to pay his debt, and I myself had conjured a nice round in the 70's. Although he found it virtually impossible to keep his ball on the planet that day, he did keep his composure, and that was admirable under the circumstances. One of the game's old aphorisms was rolling through my head as I pocketed the lucre. You do drive for show and putt for dough, but that wasn't what I was thinking. Instead, I recalled a lesser known truism, a line once delivered by a gangly assistant pro who could smote the ball into an adjoining zip code. It's true: The key shot is the tee shot.

SECTION III

Brays Island

Number 3, Par 3

Referring to Brays Island Plantation as a golf community makes about as much sense as referring to Ronald Reagan as an actor.

Sure, "The Gipper" was a celluloid mainstay in the 30's, 40's and 50's, appearing in some 60 different films. But of course his thespian career was greatly overshadowed by his political one, and to the world at large, Reagan will always be a President.

So it is at bucolic Brays Island, less than 60 miles south of Charleston. There's an excellent Ron Garl-designed golf course on the premises, one that receives as little playing pressure as virtually any course in the Lowcountry. But golf at Brays Island, pleasant and pastoral as it is, is just a single element, some might call it an ancillary element, of a vibrant

and outdoorsy community where hunting and horses hold at least as much appeal as birdies and bogeys.

Brays Island attracts a different type of member or resident than most any other development in the region. In a word, they might best be described as naturalists. This former working plantation (which produced cotton, indigo and rice, among other staples) is 5,500 acres in total. But 3,500 acres are earmarked in perpetuity as hunting and nature preserves. Man's influence on the land is subtle and restrained. With only 325 single-acre homesites in the entire plantation, just 6 percent of the property is residential. The rest is commonly owned, privately shared plantation.

There are untold hundreds of real estate develop-

ments with golf and other recreational amenities located throughout the Southeast. But none have the sportsmen's element of Brays Island. "We're unique," explains Broker in Charge Perry Harvey, who bought property in 1997, moved to the Lowcountry from Aspen in 2000 and took over the real estate sales department in 2002. "We're a real community, with many residents and members who share similar interests."

Amenities unique to Brays Island and contained in-house include the Plantation Inn with 13 suites for owners and their guests, 35 pointers in the plantation kennel ministered to by a professional dog trainer, some 45 horses at the equestrian facility with more than 100 acres of paddocks and some 60 miles of sand roads and horse trails. There's also a hunt master with a full staff of hunting professionals, a gun club featuring skeet, trap and a sporting clays course with a professional shooting instructor on staff.

Once a shooter's aim is true, there are quail, pheasant, dove, wild turkey, Chuker partridge and deer among the major field-hunting options. There are also several watercraft available for pleasure boating and fishing on the countless miles of waterway in or adjacent to the community. The lack of pressure on the golf course is part of the appeal, as is the fact there are no prearranged tee times necessary. But by the same token, it's almost a shame, considering how uniquely idyllic is the playing field.

"This course sits naturally on the site and quietly on the land," says architect Ron Garl with obvious pride. Speaking of the single most notable feature of the facility, he says, "The routing was influenced by the large live oaks and the hammocks of trees that flourish on the property. These native trees outline the playing corridors, serve as backdrops and occasionally influence the line of play."

"This course sits naturally on the site and quietly on the land," says architect Ron Garl with obvious pride.

There are several reasons the course is excellent, and paramount among them is the routing plan. Director of Golf Mike Ingram, who's been at his post since the day the course opened in 1989, explains, "We wanted the course to flow naturally around the plantation, and not be a visual intrusion. The course was designed so it would be screened from the outside like our other amenities, and not that visible or noticeable except from the interior. Some people refer to it as an 18-hole nature walk."

Taking it one step further, on the outward nine, especially, it's like a golf safari. At some point between the first fairway and green, a player loses sight of the golf house. From then on, it's a ramble in the woods, totally peaceful, with no condos, concrete or cart paths intruding. Instead, a startled golfer might come across a flock of wild turkeys or perhaps see a red-tailed hawk circling above.

Here's the Brays Island philosophy in a nutshell: "We only took down a dozen trees, if that, during construction," says Garl. Does that sound claustrophobic? No room to breathe, never mind hit spectacular slices? Perish the thought. "The holes occur naturally in open meadows or on land that had been previously cultivated for use on the plantation," continues the architect. "Our disturbance of the natural landscape was absolutely minimal."

The par-4 holes are a definite highlight, in wildly varying lengths, doglegs and directions.

There's a noticeable difference between the outward and inward nine, as the former is mostly nestled within the tree line, while the latter has a wide-open sensibility. "The front nine was a naturally undisturbed setting, while the back was part of the working plantation fields," says Garl. Even though the vistas open up, the fact is that the tee ball requires more precision on the inward nine, and the scoring average is generally a few shots higher. There are spectacular water views elsewhere on plantation property, but not necessarily on the golf course proper. Many of the hole sites were forested at the outset, and forested they shall remain.

The par-4 holes are a definite highlight, in wildly varying lengths, doglegs and directions. Most any golfer would refer to the serpentine depressions bracketing certain fairways as waste bunkers. Not the architect. "Those are native areas with sand, peppered with stalks of love grass. They're modeled after some of the great old courses of Ireland that look gnarly, wild and natural. It's in keeping with the entire Brays Island philosophy."

Working in harmony with the terrain, being stewards of the land, was the driving force in the creation of this low-lying track where tee boxes morph seamlessly into fairways, and fairways change subtly to greens. "All the living things surrounding the course, be they trees, plants, vegetation or animal life, aren't supposed to just coexist, but thrive within the golf course environment," concludes Garl.

In keeping with the understated nature of the whole plantation, and the complete lack of showiness, signage is at an absolute minimum on the golf course, as it is elsewhere on the property. To get around the course, you have to know what you're doing. And the same thing can be said for the discreet and discriminating members of this little-known facility. When they opted for life on Brays Island, they knew what they were doing, too.

Number 6, Par 3

Steve Koenig has an unusual method of marking his golf balls for identification purposes. He draws a red four-leaf clover. "I would've used green, but the first time I did it all I had handy was a red pen," he explains with a smile. He's not superstitious, but does it because it's a simple drawing. It insures he'll never hit the wrong ball, and by now everyone at his club knows the marking, and will return any errant pellet they might find while wandering the underbrush.

The clover may be a good luck charm, but it's been more than simple good fortune that Koenig has found success and accomplishment as a high-end builder and the driving force behind the remarkable Golf Club at Briar's Creek on Johns Island. It's been a combination of incredible energy devoted to the task, an unwavering commitment to his goal, a tremendous amount of hard work, and above all, vision. Along the way, there has assuredly been some luck, not all of it good, but more on that in a moment.

The Wisconsin native was educated as an industrial engineer, and joined Union Carbide thereafter. Disillusioned with the impersonal nature of big business and tired of the relocations, Koenig's corporate career lasted less than a decade. The day after he resigned, he put on a tool belt and picked up a hammer. "I was always building forts as a kid, had my first table saw at age 9, and creating structures was always part of who I was." Koenig and his family stayed put in Charleston, West Virginia, resisting Union Carbide's entreaty to come back to New York. He found success as a private-home builder, and in 1985, with the economy sagging in Appalachia, decided to make the highly desirable Charleston-to-Charleston maneuver (Kiawah Island, to get technical), and set up shop on the Carolina coast.

The move paid dividends in many ways. His wife, Sharon, thrived as an interior designer, her career fitting hand in glove with her husband's. Their kids, Scott and Sara, loved life on the coast. In direct contrast to the Charleston they left behind, their new address turned into an economic rocket. Koenig built his first Kiawah home to live in, land included, for under $200,000. His first speculative home sold for almost $800,000, inclusive of the building lot. Currently his average contract is about $2 million just for the structure itself, as the land is a separate entity. "Now it's hard to find a decent lot for the same money I sold that first spec home for," says the builder.

In the late 90's, Koenig morphed once again, from contractor to golf course developer. The impetus for creating Briar's Creek was due mostly to Paul Kimball, a home-building client of Koenig's who wondered if the builder could find an appropriate land parcel close to, but not necessarily on, Kiawah itself. "Paul and I were both members of the Kiawah Island Club, a 36-home facility with two fine courses created by Tom Fazio and Tom Watson," recalls Koenig. "As an alternative, he encouraged me to build a very private golf retreat, one that would never require tee times, or have pace-of-play issues. It was a project I got excited about. When that happens, I don't hold back."

"I just don't take the game that seriously," he explains. "To me, it's just a great way to relax."

He also gets excited on the golf course. An engineer, particularly one of German descent, might not be the first person one would equate with the term "happy-go-lucky." But Koenig has a good time on the links, his links in particular, and laughs at both good shots and bad. "I just don't take the game that seriously," he explains. "To me, it's just a great way to relax."

The developer has developed a curious but effective putting method he employs on occasion. He turns the club around, putts left-handed, and strikes the ball with the narrow blade behind the face of the putter. It's the type of nonchalant stroke players will use when they're putting for double bogey or worse. But Koenig knocked in an uphill, curling 10-footer for par while I stood by, shaking my head. "It may be unorthodox," he explains earnestly, "but I believe it helps you concentrate and put a smooth, level stroke on the ball. Besides, I think I make just as many left-handed as I do conventionally, anyway!"

Wacky putting techniques aren't all that turns him on. The engineer inside appears as he explains the intricacies of Briar's Creek state-of-the-art infrastructure. He bandies terms like "inverts," "outflow systems" and "charcoal-activated filtering" to describe various aspects of the course's irrigation and drainage methods like other players discuss birdies and bogeys.

"I feel you can look someone in the eye and tell if they're honest ..."

His golf career began casually as a Wisconsin teen. He played on the high school squad in large part, as he explains, laughing, "Because any kid that had a set of clubs was welcome to take part." He had an affinity for the game, though, claiming that in his youth he could hit the ball nearly 300 yards with the relatively unsophisticated equipment of the 1960's. Even though 40 years have passed and Koenig is now in his late 50's, he demonstrated the same power source as the round concluded. Belting two mighty balls in succession, he found the putting surface of the par-5, 550-yard finisher. The 50-foot eagle effort was 10 feet short, but with a smirk and a flourish, he turned southpaw once again, rolling home the birdie with the back of the blade. Bravo.

"I feel you can look someone in the eye and tell if they're honest," explains the managing partner, referring to the first time he met his Briar's Creek partner, Ed Myrick. Myrick owned the land on Johns Island that Koenig coveted. At the time, it was a quirky combination of tomato, cucumber and sunflower fields, as well as a migrant workers camp. But Koenig thought it would make the perfect golf retreat.

"Beyond that, I know you can't be successful buying and selling produce on a wholesale level like Ed is unless your word is your bond. I trusted him implicitly, and that trust never faltered." Maybe so, but when Koenig put up well over a million dollars of his own money with nothing more than a handshake agreement with Myrick, his attorneys were continually admonishing him as reckless and irresponsible. What the lawyers didn't understand is the kismet between the two men. During their initial meeting, the first time the pair had ever laid eyes on each other, they each brought along their sons, unannounced. Not only did Steve and Ed get along from the start, but their young-adult sons, Scott Koenig and Eddie Myrick, did also. The principals were impressed with each other's family values, business acumen and desire to minimize the impact on the land. Myrick had rebuffed numerous offers to develop the parcel previously, but felt that Koenig was the right man for the job. The deal began to take shape.

Koenig scored a coup by hiring renowned architect Rees Jones to design the golf course, but that was a trifling matter in comparison to finding the well-heeled members necessary to fund the project. There was nothing to show prospects other than dirt roads, fields of produce, busted farm equipment and other assorted detritus blighting the landscape. But there was also abundant wildlife, ornithological in particular, and water vistas from the higher points on the property. His passionate and enthusiastic vision of what would eventually sprout from the land convinced a score of otherwise-sober individuals to pony up the $700,000 initiation fee to become Founding Members of Briar's Creek.

Koenig scored a coup by hiring renowned architect Rees Jones to design the golf course, but that was a trifling matter in comparison to finding the well-heeled members necessary to fund the project.

"Steve was undoubtedly the engine driving the train that got this project off of the ground," explains Rees Jones. "I admire the man on many levels. He's very honest, direct and honorable. He's just a good guy." Jones found Koenig easy to work with, in large part because their vision of the project was similar. "It certainly didn't hurt that we had such a tremendous piece of land to work with in making this course a reality," concludes the architect.

One of the most poignant parts of the Koenig story is Sharon's decade-long battle with breast cancer. Besides the optimism and focus he brings to projects, another of Koenig's assets is a seemingly limitless supply of energy, a quality that limits his sleep to perhaps four hours a night. But turning the golf dream into reality while his wife of more than 30 years was struggling against a relentless opponent was a sobering and draining experience. "Sharon was extremely supportive of Briar's Creek, as she was of all my endeavors and all the children's pursuits," explains the widower, who lost his wife in mid winter of 2003. For the first time, Koenig loses his easy smile, and speaks solemnly and slowly about the girl he married the day before their college graduation. "We never gave up hope. We didn't realize it would be terminal until the last few years. My brother Paul moved here from Houston to work with me, which allowed me to take time off as needed. In a way, it was easy to continue along, because she wanted the project to come to fruition as much as any of us. We have wonderful photos of our opening evening together here at Briar's Creek, with my family and all of the founding members present."

A simple and thoughtful gesture by members' wives continues to resonate with the managing partner several years later. "They named the women's club championship The Sharon Cup in honor of my wife. That first year, the women's club champion, Donna Bailey, brought the trophy over to our house, filled with flowers, and presented it to Sharon."

A simple and thoughtful gesture by members' wives continues to resonate with the managing partner several years later.

Though Sharon is gone, the family remains close. The kids, nearing and just past 30, work for their father. Scott is a project manager for Koenig Construction. He hangs around Briar's Creek enough to maintain a 3 handicap and visit with his younger sister, Sara, the membership coordinator at the club. Scott and his wife, Suzanne, have two little ones, Scott Christopher and Anneliese, who revel in their grandfather's attentions.

Steve relocated to Johns Island not long ago, building and moving into an understated lakefront home on the Briar's Creek property. It'll be the first time in two decades he won't have a Kiawah Island address. "I want to show the membership how committed I am to this project, and what better way to do so than to live on site? Besides, considering our goal is to keep this property as close to nature as possible, it would be hard to find a nicer place to live."

Earlier that same day, Koenig professed a desire to take some time off down the road after the club is more firmly established, after the real estate component is really in place. "Rees Jones has inspired me to go out and visit some of the great golf venues in the world. I want to go out and play a bunch of the great courses," he said.

It's a noble goal, if an ironic one. Because of the hard work and undiminished enthusiasm he brought to the creation of the Golf Club at Briar's Creek, one of the very best venues in the nation is at his beck and call. Quite literally, it's in Steve Koenig's backyard.

Briar's Creek

Number 4, Par 3

snapshot of the attention to detail that is the hallmark of the Golf Club at Briar's Creek: Fifteen styles of bunker rakes were rejected before management settled on the one they liked the best. It's a beauty, no doubt. Light handle, wide tines and with a squeegee-like rubber strip opposite the tines to efficiently remove sand that was splashed onto the green from the bunker. And you thought your club had thought of everything.

No, the rumors are unfounded. Contrary to popular belief, you needn't have appeared on either the cover of Forbes or Fortune to be a member here, although if you had, you'd be in fast company. But the fact is that the Golf Club at Briar's Creek was conceived not so much as an exclusive private club, but more as a golf retreat. It's no accident this tranquil 915-acre parcel sits midway between Kiawah Island and the Charleston Executive Airport. The former is full of $5 million and $10 million mansions, the latter home base for the private-jet set. Get the picture?

This Rees Jones beauty is laid out on more than 300

acres, with just a dozen random homesites dotting the property. Clearly, golf is the absolute focus, as the real estate component of the property is adjacent to but separate from the playing fields. Eventually, as many as 90 homes will be built on the 900-plus acres allotted for this task, with plenty of open spaces, so low density, low impact is the watchword.

This Rees Jones beauty is laid out on more than 300 acres, with just a dozen random homesites dotting the property.

Head Professional Chris Edwards is an enthusiastic proponent of this, his home turf. The Englishman has held the top job at Briar's Creek since the first foursome strode to the first tee on opening day. He speaks eloquently about the unpretentious layout. "When I think of the epitome of 'class,' I think of confident, subtle and understated. Briar's Creek was designed with this subtle understatement."

The longtime pro came to Johns Island shortly after

Number 2, Par 3

play concluded at the 2001 PGA Championship at the Atlanta Athletic Club, where he served as head professional. He won't be the host pro at a major championship anytime soon, certainly not at Briar's Creek. But that hardly seems to matter. "It would have been an easier task to have created a memorable golf course with unnatural or unfair barriers. It is far more difficult to create the understated and simple challenges that rely on the purity of nature, the changing breezes, the fingers of marshland and those majestic oaks to create that experience. Rees Jones has achieved this intrigue by relying on the golfer's imagination and not his ego."

"It is far more difficult to create the understated and simple challenges that rely on the purity of nature, the changing breezes, the fingers of marshland and those majestic oaks to create that experience."
– Head Professional Chris Edwards

Briar's Creek is a 7,100-yard nature walk. It's as quiet and pastoral a golf course as you'll find in the Lowcountry, or just about any country. Massive tree canopies, broad saltwater estuaries, the Kiawah River and Briar's Creek itself make for an organically scenic backdrop to a golf course that offers one impressive hole after another. Step back to the blacks if you're game enough to deal with more than 7,000 yards of rolling terrain. From the blue tees, 6,760 yards and a 136 slope rating will be more than enough for most players. Step forward to the whites at 6,300 yards if so inclined. The number of forced carries remains the same, but the yardage required to find safe purchase on the other side is reduced, as is the slope rating, now down to 126.

Certainly one of the most taxing aspects of the golf course are these forced carries that exist from tee to fairway throughout the property. Nowhere is the challenge more dramatic than on the penultimate hole. This is a 200-plus-yard par 3 from the blue markers, where just the wetland itself widens from 140 to 175 yards, depending on where it's crossed. This hole is a heart-thumper for the average golfer, but many of the other wetland carries are made a bit easier, once again because of attention to detail. On every par 4 and par 5 with a forced carry, there are

two numbers on the tee box marker. The first is the length of the hole, and the underlying number is the length of the carry over the obstacle. This serves a dual purpose. First, it provides the type of hard information that most players crave. Secondly, the carries are a bit of a visual illusion, and appear to be longer and more daunting than they actually are. Knowing that to clear the vegetation might only be 180 yards, for example, makes for a slightly looser grip on the driver, particularly when the angle and direction of the hole make it look closer to 200 yards instead.

Certainly one of the most taxing aspects of the golf course are these forced carries that exist from tee to fairway throughout the property.

"The carries are effectively incorporated into the design, because they are almost all off the tee," says the architect. "If a player chooses the appropriate tee box for their ability level, much of the difficulty is mitigated. There are relatively few carries from fairway to green, which is a much more difficult proposition." Other than several of the par-3 holes, the only carries a player must negotiate from fairway to green are on the closing holes on each side. The ninth and 18th, a 370-yard par 4 and a 550-yard par 5, respectively, are arguably the most spectacular holes on the course.

A weir system, which in layman's terms is best described as a mini-dam, helps to trap tidal waters that come from the ocean. From the Atlantic, they move into the Stono and then Kiawah rivers, then into Briar's Creek and some of the extensive marshes found on the outward nine. Without this engineering mechanism, the wetlands would drain dry. The wonderful variety of birdlife that call Briar's Creek home would disappear.

"The technical challenges in building the course were relatively straightforward," says Jones. "We had to work around the wonderful specimen trees and some of the wetlands, but it all worked out quite well." So well that it's the first course in South Carolina to be named as a certified Silver Signature Sanctuary by Audubon International.

"Incorporating all the natural features, routing through the wetland and finishing both nines on Briar's Creek itself were the real challenges," claims the onetime Architect of the Year as named by Golf

World Magazine. And the challenge for the players is keeping the ball out of the ubiquitous marshland.

"Briar's Creek represents an impressive step in the career of Rees Jones," says Brad Klein earnestly. The architecture editor at Golfweek elaborates, claiming, "Here he has dispensed with his symmetrical containment mounding and embraced instead a retro-classic sensibility. There are elements of Raynor-like falloffs and steep, Tillinghast-style greenside bunkering throughout the property. The theme is established at the first hole, a wonderful short par 4, and culminates at the 18th in one of the most strategically diverse par 5's I have seen in modern golf. There are true optional routes on this hole, with all classes of golfers presented with alternative paths on the drive, second shot and approach across the marsh."

> *"Briar's Creek represents an impressive step in the career of Rees Jones."*
> *– Brad Klein, Golfweek*

"There's lots of variety on the course, lots of angles in play, plenty of places you can choose to carry more of the hazard for a shorter shot into the green," explains Jones. "Both nines finish in spectacular fashion, in my opinion. You always hope to build a course that finishes in a crescendo, and I really think we accomplished that here. The closing holes, the 15th though 18th, are really dramatic." Jones takes great satisfaction in having built a course that won't demoralize a neophyte playing from the appropriate tees, but can also offer a staunch challenge to the scratch player.

This praiseworthy layout maintains a low profile on the landscape, with almost nothing in the way of artificiality, mounding or other intrusions. Likewise, the club itself maintains an equally low profile, but the golf world has taken notice regardless. Perhaps the most prestigious award the Golf Club at Briar's Creek has received to date is being named among the top 45 golf courses created since 1959 by the panelists at GOLF Magazine. Although some might argue that being tabbed by Golf Digest as Best New Private Club of 2002 is an equal accolade. But don't expect awards or attention to bring the course into the general consciousness. "In 10 or 15 years, we fully expect that most golfers in the world still won't know we exist," explains managing partner Steve Koenig.

This Vagabond Golfer is fortunate to have had a comprehensive look at this excellent but unassuming facility, the province of a privileged few. It's easy to see why Briar's Creek, upon completion, immediately took a position near the top of the pecking order. Though only a few years old, it's already a Charleston classic.

> *This praiseworthy layout maintains a low profile on the landscape, with almost nothing in the way of artificiality, mounding or other intrusions.*

Number 18, Par 5

If I'm not taking a divot somewhere in the Lowcountry, there's an excellent chance I'm taking a chairlift somewhere in snow country. Sliding down snow-covered hills has been an elemental part of my life for some 30 years now, and I've got the closet full of skis, snowboards, knee braces and crutches to prove it.

I've got the closet full of skis, snowboards, knee braces and crutches to prove it.

Though I spend far more time in soft spikes than ski boots, my skill level seems to be higher on the snow. It must be something in my physiology or genetic makeup. For some reason, descending a 30-degree pitch on a narrow, wooded trail affords less angst than executing a 30-yard pitch over water.

In any event, here is a rudimentary point-by-point comparison between two of my favorite avocations: Neither sport is what can be considered a cheap thrill. Both the equipment required and access to the playground in question can be major expenditures. This isn't the time or place to scrutinize the MSRP of every piece of equipment necessary to be well equipped in either discipline. We'll just say that, in broad terms, a basic beginner ski package consisting of skis, bindings, boots and poles, or a starter set of a dozen or so clubs, a golf bag and shoes is around $500. You can equip decently in either sport for $1,000 or $1,500. And real enthusiasts can easily spend $1,000 more in either discipline for the best of the best. Of course, these are just the basics. Golfers have the most prohibitive ongoing expense, the ammo required to play, and depending on the skill level (or lack thereof), those $4 sleeves of Titleist balls can really add up over time. Depending on the mental acuity or dexterity of the skier in question, goggles, gloves, hats, neck warmers, sunglasses, etc., can be considered "disposable" items as well. One word of advice from someone who's been there time and time again: Keep careful inventory of your stuff as you exit the ski lodge and don't fiddle with your accessories on the chairlift!

While equipment itself is something of a wash in terms of prices, golf becomes prohibitively more expensive in the actual doing. Seventy dollars for a daily ski pass is outrageous, even at the swankiest ski hill. But that same expenditure won't even allow you to sniff the cheapest twilight walker's shoulder-season-package-deal greens fee at any marquee golf destination. Here's another way of looking at it: A five-day ski pass at a top-end destination like Colorado's Vail is just about the same price as a five-hour round will cost at Pebble Beach. Loyalty to a single golf venue offers nothing in the way of a price break, either. A season pass to a ski hill is usually in the $800-$1,200 range. Membership in a nice country club is more along the lines of $5,000-$7,000 a year, not counting an initiation fee that is often well into five figures, occasionally more than that.

They're similar in that they both offer the prospect of abject humiliation from the get-go.

Learning these respective sports? They're similar in that they both offer the prospect of abject humiliation from the get-go, although those with a modicum of coordination can zoom from total incompetence to lower-level mediocrity in short order. While neophytes sometimes swing a golf club much too close to their playing companions, quickly develop blisters and often neglect to use sunscreen, skiing is surely more dangerous, by and large. Sliding downhill as a cautious intermediate is a realistic goal for most folks nimble and spirited enough to attempt the sport. The same cannot be said for golf though, where untold legions of devotees can never develop the rudimentary skills necessary to slide down into a double-digit score for 18 holes. But the embarrassment factor is similar. Every skier on earth has been splayed under a chairlift at one time or another, poles, hat, goggles and other accoutrements scattered in disarray on the hill in what's known in the vernacular as a "yard sale," enduring hoots and catcalls from those riding above. Newbie golfers swing and miss, hit the ball sideways and knock 10-foot putts 25 feet past the hole. It's just the price of learning a new and foreign discipline.

On the subject of humiliation though, one hard-to-believe personal incident stands out. It was my first day on skis. I had gotten comfortable descending, turning and stopping that morning on the beginner's slope, or "bunny hill." The mode of transport was a surface lift called a T-bar, which took wobbly skiers from bottom to top. After lunch I got ambitious and decided to seek higher ground farther up the mountain. My very first chairlift ride was solo. Near the top of the lift I saw a sign that said "Exit Here." So I lifted the safety bar and jumped, not realizing the sign actually meant prepare to exit a couple of seconds later by sliding down the ramp. I can still see the look on the lift attendant's face when he came bolting out of his little kiosk and asked me what I was doing. There I was, a dopey 14-year-old caught in the protective netting underneath the lift like a fly in a spider's web, equipment and limbs akimbo. "It said 'Exit Here,' so I did," was all I could mumble. Thankfully, I've never endured a parallel incident of complete and utter ineptitude on the golf course.

Flatlanders might think that skiing isn't really a workout, because the gist of the sport is sliding downhill with gravity doing the work. Nothing could be further from the truth. Just getting your ski boots on and buckled expends the same energy needed to play a par 5 into a stiff breeze. Loading the gear onto the ski rack and into the trunk burns the same amount of calories as playing back-to-back ocean-side par 3's. The layering, hauling, clomping about and lift-line shuffling add up. By the time a skier is poised at the top of the hill, anticipating the first turns of the day, he's expended the same amount of effort as a cart-riding golfer has standing on the 15th tee.

Thankfully, I've never endured a parallel incident of complete and utter ineptitude on the golf course.

To the legions who don't know a telemark turn from a T-bar, all ski mountains must look alike. From personal experience, I can assure you there are vast differences between Montana's Big Sky and Big Mountain, New England's Sugarbush and Sugarloaf, and Utah's Snowbird and Snowbasin. But to the uninitiated, they are all just big white hills, dotted with trees and chairlifts. Of course, the golf cynic can turn the tables, claiming that every course is just a field of green with 18 separate flags sticking out of the ground. But that's simplistic to the point of absurd. Pine Valley bears no resemblance to Pebble Beach, which is entirely different from Pinehurst No. 2, which is wholly unlike Prairie Dunes, which has nothing in common with Portmarnock.

Clothing in golf takes three basic forms. There are the classy dressers among us, usually few and far between. Think of Tour pros like Tommy Armour III or Fred Couples. Secondly, there is the athletic look popularized by Tiger Woods and David Duval in recent years, though not one in 50 golfers has the requisite physique to pull off this fashion sensibility effectively. Finally, there's the Duffy Waldorf aesthetic, a rumpled, casual look adopted by the overwhelming majority of players, a look that screams "golf is war." Granted, there's an entire universe of outerwear, rain gear and wind wear. But these three basic looks are the bread and butter of golf fashion, which is itself an expression that the truly fashion conscious among us might consider an oxymoron. But skiwear? That's a whole different story.

Finally, there's the Duffy Waldorf aesthetic, a rumpled, casual look adopted by the overwhelming majority of players, a look that screams "golf is war."

How do we even begin to count the various permutations of what is basically a snowsuit? There are one-piece outfits, matching ensembles, shells, vests, pullovers and parkas. Snowmen use polypropylene, Gore-Tex, microfibers, fleece, goose down, wool, PrimaLoft, Spylon, Dermizax and a dozen other natural and/or synthetic materials that provide both warmth and enough flexibility so the skier doesn't resemble the Michelin Man.

Lastly and most importantly is the thrill or pleasure factor. How to compare? I've been fortunate to make an ace, hole out for eagle from some 200 yards, and chip in on consecutive holes. I've also glided through unbroken fields blanketed with three feet of fresh powder, zipped and dipped through thick evergreens on a sparkling day and landed safely on a cushion of snow after leaping from a rock promontory.

On the other hand, I've been humiliated when leaving consecutive bunker shots in the hazard, ruined my hand while hitting down on an unseen tree root and been emasculated by adolescents who routinely drive the ball 50 yards farther than my best efforts. I've also had my knee wrapped around a tree so grotesquely a ski companion had to come release my binding. I've been rescued deep in the woods and well out-of-bounds by a ski patrolman who shepherded both my daughter and me to safety on a snowmobile, and been stuck for what seemed like an eternity on a chairlift directly in a snowmaking gun's line of fire.

I've enjoyed them both for decades, and hope to continue pursuing the perfect turn and effortless swing for years to come.

Through the good, the bad and the ugly, I've enjoyed them both for decades, and hope to continue pursuing the perfect turn and effortless swing for years to come. Here's one more difference worth noting: I wish I'd started chasing golf balls earlier in life, and hope to continue chasing chairlifts much later in life. Lastly, not only are both pastimes about as much fun as you can have fully clothed, but by the same token, just as in matters libidinous or licentious, skill is not a prerequisite for enjoyment.

Let's say you're one of the most accomplished and prominent lawyers in your city, not to mention the state, not to mention the nation. Let's say you helped to litigate settlements in the hundreds of billions (no misprint there) against the big tobacco and asbestos industries. Besides righting the wrongs of huge corporations and getting the injured and aggrieved their just due, the financial remuneration resulting from the successful lawsuits was a "set-for-life" figure. Let's say you're one of two managing partners in a firm employing more than fifty attorneys, with a support staff of 400. Would you have the time and inclination to pursue other business interests also? I ask Joe Rice this question as we sit in a beautiful glass-and-brass bistro called Zinc, on the ground floor of his office building near Patriots Point. We're on the patio, overlooking Charleston Harbor on a dazzling afternoon, the aircraft carrier USS Yorktown looming in the middle distance, seemingly a mid iron away. "As a matter of fact I do," Rice says, with a small smile. "You're sitting in one now."

Yes, Rice is an attorney. He's also a club owner, restaurateur, tavern owner, event promoter, sports-management principal, hotel owner and who knows what else? The 50-ish attorney is also a golf course entrepreneur and the driving force behind one of Charleston's most-talked-about new private clubs, Bulls Bay. "I stay pretty busy," admits Rice. Yeah, and Wayne Gretzky could skate a little.

Rice's involvement in the creation of Bulls Bay Golf Club is a direct result of his love for the sport. Not golf, horseback riding. "I met golf course-architect Mike Strantz one day while riding horses. Prior to that, I had been approached by a man named Larry McKay, who wanted me to become one of about 25 partners in a golf course project."

The land had been selected, and Strantz was on board as the architect. But eventually, the plans unraveled. There were constraints on time, permitting, money and deadlines, the type of roadblocks that virtually every nascent golf course project endures, and that meant the deal had to be restructured. When McKay asked Rice if he would be interested in taking on a larger role in the project, the attorney decided to size up the architect that had been chosen for the job. "Strantz and his design consultant, Forrest Fezler, met me at the property, and we rode our horses together, checking out the landscape." The former tomato farm in Awendaw, about half an hour north of downtown Charleston, was a morass of woods, open fields and irrigation ditches. It was also as flat as a tabletop.

Yes, Rice is an attorney. He's also a club owner, restaurateur, tavern owner, event promoter, sports-management principal, hotel owner and who knows what else?

"Strantz told me I wouldn't understand the concept of what he had in mind unless he showed me some representative courses. So we went to Long Island and played at National Golf Links and Shinnecock Hills." Rice was incredulous that the architect would attempt to mimic the East End's rolling terrain and dramatic elevation changes in the Carolina Lowcountry. But after seeing the avant-garde Strantz style showcased at North Carolina's Tobacco Road and Tot Hill, he decided to buy into the program. "He told me he could replicate the look and feel of those gems on Long Island, and I just shrugged and said let's do it."

> *"It was just too good," he says with a laugh. "I knew we had something special, and it deserved the type of stewardship you'll only see at a private facility."*

Rice decided to take on the project by himself. He refunded the cash outlay to the individual partners and offered them each founding-membership status in the club. Although Bulls Bay was originally slated as a semiprivate facility, Rice decided to turn it totally private after seeing what was transpiring on the land.

"It was just too good," he says with a laugh. "I knew we had something special, and it deserved the type of stewardship you'll only see at a private facility."

Rice has a business history of surrounding himself with competent partners and letting them go about their business. He has the humility and foresight to understand that, while he may be an expert in the law, his expertise doesn't extend into every other field of business. "I try to hook up with good people in business ventures that make sense and then stay out of their way." But Bulls Bay was a change from that basic philosophy. "I figured I'd just go ahead and do it and not have to do it by committee." Rice put his trust in Strantz, intrigued that the architect's original background wasn't in golf, wasn't in turf school or agronomy, but actually art. "He's an accomplished artisan who does magnificent work. He draws every hole before he touches the land, and every drawing is worth framing." Rice also was heartened by the fact that Strantz wanted some acreage on the property as part of the deal. "I figured if he wanted to set up his permanent residence practically on site, he'd put everything he had into the project, and I was right."

Strantz returns the compliment to Rice. "Joe was probably one of the best clients we've ever had. He is very successful. He doesn't have any problems with his own confidence and he certainly doesn't have an inferiority complex," explains the 1998 Architect of the Year as chosen by Golf World Magazine. "So his approach was, 'I hired you guys to build a golf course, so you guys build the golf course.' Now, he had some guidelines. He obvious-

ly didn't want it to play overly difficult, but he also wanted a demanding test. Anytime you work for any client, you have to keep their wishes in the forefront. But it was great working with Joe because he was very clear about what he wanted."

Rice has very few regrets about the way the project turned out. "I suppose we should've started with bent grass greens," he offers. "When we thought it was going to be a public-access course, we decided to use Bermuda grass, and then had to rip them out and go for bent grass later on. Other than that, it's gone along just fine."

Bulls Bay is a club that's a fine reflection of its principal. "Joe invited about 20 friends, all membership prospects, out to the club," recalls Reid Nelson, who was impressed enough to become a founding member. "The course was finished and it was the first time an entire group was going to play all 18 holes. He said, 'Guys, if you want to play golf, this is where you should be a member. If you want to go swimming or play tennis, you should go somewhere else. We're going to play golf, play cards, drink a little liquor and smoke cigars. And if you want to wear jeans and cowboy boots in the clubhouse, that's okay too.' There was no pretense involved and that was really appealing."

That easygoing philosophy, along with Rice's far-flung legal connections, has increased Bulls Bay's membership steadily. "In my work, I've met and befriended lawyers from around the country," says Rice. "Many of them have joined the club; in large part, because Charleston is such an attractive part of the country." A quarter of the current members live outside the immediate area, a number that might move to a third as the club looks for a full complement of 350 members in total.

> *That easygoing philosophy, along with Rice's far-flung legal connections, has increased Bulls Bay's membership steadily.*

Being an attorney can be rewarding work, lucrative work and challenging work, but it's undoubtedly indoor work, and Rice prefers to be outdoors. He rides his horses, rides his Harley, likes to fish and spends time on his boat, called Rice Quarters. Not quick to offer details other than that the vessel is often docked in the Caribbean, one can only surmise it's just a wee bit bigger than a Boston Whaler. While he loves the game of golf, his ability and devotion are erratic and sporadic, respectively. "My handicap is in the mid teens," he explains with a shrug. Not hard to understand, because despite his head-honcho status at Bulls Bay, and memberships at Daniel Island, Secession Club down in Beaufort, the University Club in Columbia and a partnership interest at Raspberry Falls in Virginia, he only takes to the links a couple of times a month.

Because everything is relative, Joe qualifies as the avid golfer in the family. His wife, Lisa, loves the boat, referring to it as "my golf course," and his 20-something daughter, Ann E., not only followed her father to the University of South Carolina, but to the saddle as well. "Our daughter shows horses competitively in the hunter/jumper area throughout the Southeast," explains Rice, a hint of pride in his voice for the first and only time in our meeting.

Charleston's Forrest Edwards, a mortgage banker and longtime friend of the attorney since the two were fraternity brothers at the University of South Carolina more than 30 years ago, says, "Joe is a very competitive guy, on the golf course and off. When you lose, it might not be on the course itself, but because of the stakes he'll set on the first tee." Edwards continues with high praise for his college buddy, "Over the decades together, I can count on one hand how many times I've seen him in a coat and tie. He's just a comfortable, casual guy, unpretentious and with a heart of gold. It would be hard to find a guy who has had his type of success that's more down to earth."

"Someone once said to me that you only live once, but if you do it right the first time, it's okay,"
– Joe Rice

"Someone once said to me that you only live once, but if you do it right the first time, it's okay," says Rice by way of goodbye, chuckling as he stands up to shake hands. He has a full slate of appointments to keep. There are conference calls in the offing, a first-ever golf trip to Scotland on the near horizon, dozens of matters both personal and professional to attend to in short order. Then Joe Rice, Man in Full, leaves the building.

Bulls Bay

Number 7, Par 3

*I*t's one of the great clichés of the golf writing business. "This course is unlike any other in the area."

Well in this case it's more than hype. Bulls Bay is truly unlike any course in greater Charleston, or any course in the Carolina Lowcountry, for that matter. This fact is self-evident as you drive into the property, the road turns and you catch the first glimpse of the stately clubhouse perched in the sky above the property. In the scheme of things, 75 or 80 feet above sea level doesn't sound like much. But in this part of the world the topography is like a tabletop, and Bulls Bay affords a sensibility that simply doesn't exist anywhere else. The rustic logo of a bull's skull sets the tone as you drive through the gate. Seeing the acreage stretching vertically as well as horizontally upon approach is reminiscent of courses in the Rocky Mountains. It's a unique perspective, to say the least. Call it "Carolina meets Colorado."

It's a unique perspective, to say the least. Call it "Carolina meets Colorado."

"You build the clubhouse up on the highest central point and let golf surround it," says architect Mike Strantz, explaining his philosophy. "You're literally looking at that vista for anywhere from 12 to 16 golf holes. I think that's what makes the club unique. The biggest thing was the long-range vistas over Bulls Bay and Bull Island, out to Capers Island. Couple that

Number 14, Par 3

with the fact that it's so difficult to put the clubhouse and the central focus of a golf course on the coast, because of all the environmental regulations. It just made sense to come back into the interior of the property where there was nothing but tomato fields. How else would you take advantage of that entire vista but to start building it up where you could see it?"

"The topography change is undoubtedly our calling card ..."

Terry Florence is one of the area's most enduring golf figures, with more than 30 years of experience in greater Charleston. He left Wild Dunes after a 20-year stint to take Bulls Bay by the horns on opening day, in 2002. "The topography change is undoubtedly our calling card," begins the director of golf. "To have this beautiful clubhouse sitting on top of an 80-foot dune, with panoramic views of 14 holes of the course stretched out in front of you, with views of the Intracoastal Waterway and four separate islands behind that, it's just not something you see in this part of the world."

The dynamism of the course goes beyond the elevated driving range, which a pragmatist understands affords a greater sense of power than truly exists. It's beyond the towering tee boxes providing hang time for a booming drive, or the near-vertical approach shots required to reach the ninth and 18th greens in regulation. The course is, in a literal sense, a work of art. Not surprising, considering that architect Mike Strantz is actually an artist who expresses himself with great individualism on this living, growing, green grass canvas. At certain moments during the round, the course looks like a painting. The sweep of the fairways, the curve of the bunkering and the placement of the love grass all lend an artistic feel to the playing field.

"Strantz envisioned the course with the massive mound and clubhouse as the focal point," continues Florence. "He built a trio of tee complexes and green complexes at the apex of the property, and then routed the course away from the high point into different directions, different corners of the acreage. The course meanders to and from the high point several different times during the round, and the end result is a wonderful ebb and flow to a round of golf. It makes for a dramatic and thoroughly enjoyable experience."

There are "rounds within the round" at Bulls Bay. There are marsh holes, holes routed through woodlands, many holes where the clubhouse is in plain view, lording over the grounds. There are other corners, either among the water hazards or within the hardwoods and vegetation where the defining structure of the property is just a distant memory. There are links-style holes, holes that are buffeted by a near-constant wind, and a demanding series of par-3 holes that require great precision. But among the essential features of Bulls Bay is a wide-open sensibility off the tee, and a series of rolling, heaving greens that grow more demanding as the round progresses.

"Artistically speaking, any time you open up a piece of ground as wide as this one, you have to make things big because if you try to make small features, like little humps and bumps, it just doesn't work visually," says Strantz. "Given the windy conditions out here, I thought the only way to make the course playable and a reasonable test for the good player concurrently was to create wide fairways that are accessible to any type of shot. There is unlimited room on most holes for any shape of shot to be started off the tee. Though the landing areas are wide, you still need to be in the right spot to have the best chance to score. You need to put the golf ball in certain places and those places change all the time, depending on the contour of the green and where the pins are located that day."

The greens mimic the drama of the terrain, which is part of the architectural genius of the course.

The greens mimic the drama of the terrain, which is part of the architectural genius of the course. The opening holes feature greens that are relatively flat and straightforward, but before too long the putting surfaces begin to heave, buckle and tilt like a storm-tossed ship at sea. The 11th affords a perfect example. It's a challenging dogleg of 415 yards around a sizeable retention pond with some of the clearest water in Charleston County. There's considerable trouble to be found on both the tee shot and approach, but the fun (and head shaking) truly begins on the green. Sixty-five yards in length, the green might best be described as a "reverse Biarritz." Instead of a deep valley, this putting surface is bisected horizontally by a large, rolling hump that traverses the width of the green. Imagine a rectangular table placemat that's lying on top of a rolling pin.

The challenge goes well beyond the greens though, tough as many of them can be. Perhaps the most daunting task on the 6,560-yard course (which can stretch to 7,150 yards for the masters or masochists among us) is found on the 13th. This 560-yard par 5 begins back among the retention ponds on the northeast corner, with no view of the club headquarters high on the hill. Chasing down the tee shot on this double-dogleg right affords a wonderful view of the clubhouse, but no time to admire the visual trickery of the architect. One must deliver an equally powerful second shot to get the ball beyond the tree line bracketing the right side of the fairway. In so doing, there'll be a clear look at the sloping green, fronted by the stream that's snaked along laterally the length of the fairway. Three solid shots are required for a legitimate birdie putt. Falter on any one of them and it will undoubtedly be an unlucky 13th.

Imagine a rectangular table placemat that's lying on top of a rolling pin.

This is in direct contrast to the par-5 fourth hole, on both the other end of the property and the difficulty scale. This 510-yard confection close by the Intracoastal offers a classic risk/reward scenario. Take the aggressive route from the tee, launch the ball over what seems to be acres of vegetation, bounce it onto the short grass and have a mid or even short iron to the green. Or play to the left, avoiding the trouble from the tee, and plod your way home in regulation.

"You can turn it loose here," concludes Strantz, referring to the driver-friendly nature of the terrain. "You don't feel anxious standing up on the tee, which is a nice feature. I believe that's the way it had to be designed, because when the wind gets up out here, you're going to be intimidated."

Intimidated? Maybe, depending on whether the breeze is a flutter or a force. Exhilarated? At Bulls Bay, that's an everyday occurrence.

Number 11, Par 4

An interviewer's tools of the trade: a list of pertinent questions, a micro-cassette recorder, an open mind, a notebook and pen. But in this strange and melancholy scenario, it was the subject, and not the questioner, who did the writing.

The Awendaw home of Mike and Heidi Strantz is spectacular. It's like a Soho loft in a forest clearing, like an industrial ware-house on stilts, set somewhat discordant-ly but majestically upon the Ponderosa. It lords imperiously amid the woods and pastures of this quiet horse farm property, perhaps 15 miles north-east of downtown Charleston, and little more than a mile from the Bulls Bay golf course, one of Mike's most highly regarded designs. The dwelling - airy, spare, filled with brickwork, big windows and even bigger views of miles of marsh-land - is an attention-getter. It's not unlike the archi-tect's courses, which can be loved or loathed, depend-ing on the golfer, but are impossible to ignore.

The tongue cancer he's been battling for years has rendered him virtually speechless.

His golf course concepts might be controversial. But the outpouring of affection and concern for the terribly ill architect is universal. The tongue cancer he's been battling for years has rendered him virtual-ly speechless. He communicates mostly with his eyes, by nodding, shaking his head, smiling, shrugging or writing on a whiteboard. The fact that Strantz is unable to speak is almost ironic, because his arresting golf course designs speak volumes. They are bold, imaginative and striking, like their dream home,

which they first occupied late in 2004.

Bulls Bay is among the most conspicuous courses in greater Charleston, due in large part to the Strantz-conceived, manmade mini-mountain, perched 75 feet above sea level, where the clubhouse is located. At a glance, a visitor might equate their new digs, perched high in the air, as a tribute to the nearby club-house, which is both a launching point and locus of several of the wonderful golf holes. Stunning it may be, but the design rationale was also utilitari-an. "It's building code," explains Heidi, with a smile. The petite blonde married her "latent hip-pie," as she once referred to him, more than 25 years ago. Heidi is 50ish, but extremely youthful in bearing and demeanor. Her bob of hair and facial angularity offer just a hint of resemblance to Angie Dickinson. Understandably, she does all of the talking. "The Intracoastal Waterway is two miles out," she continues, referencing the vast expanse of golden marshland beyond their back deck. "We're considered first threat in a hurricane, and we have to be up at least 18 feet above sea level. We built it 22 feet high."

Commenting on the interior brickwork featured prominently in the main living space, Heidi says, "The builder put in one wall of brick, then asked us if he should continue. Mike told him to do the whole room. I love the way it turned out," she exclaims, chuckling. "But I don't think I would've been as brave."

Brave is the operative word, and not just because Strantz is unafraid to pepper his iconoclastic designs with curious features rarely seen in modern architec-ture. He's been known to tuck greens down in glens and atop sand hills, or build them exponentially wider than they are deep. He's constructed them in such close proximity to rock features that a poor approach will go rocketing off the granite into oblivion. He's built bunkers with 30-foot walls, and putting surfaces that roiled and shimmied to the point that walking on them, never mind putting on them, was a chore. But in this case, brave means battling an insidious and sinister disease, an "old man's disease," in the words of his attentive wife, that struck him like a lightning bolt in his mid-40's. Brave is setting up coast-to-coast chemotherapy sessions so he could fight back against the cancer both at home in Charleston and in California, where he dragged himself to work on renovation projects in San Jose and on the Monterey Peninsula. "I think it's fair to say he has the admiration of every member of the Monterey Peninsula Country Club," says Heidi earnestly. "I think people are amazed, the doctors especially, by Mike's energy level. Despite radiation treatments, chemo, surgeries. He keeps going."

Mike and Heidi met and married back in their hometown of Toledo, Ohio. The Midwesterners discovered Charleston when Strantz was pulling duty at Wild Dunes, working for Tom Fazio on the Harbor Course. "We were in Florida, Hilton Head, Oklahoma, then back to Florida, as Mike worked on various golf projects," says Heidi, who shares her husband's affection for horses. "When we came here, our oldest daughter, Dana, who's now out of college, was 2. I said, 'I like it here. I'm staying.' So we did!"

The Strantz family grew to love Charleston like all thinking people do, enamored of the climate, the culture, the graciousness of the citizenry.

The Strantz family grew to love Charleston like all thinking people do, enamored of the climate, the culture, the graciousness of the citizenry. As an artist and painter, in addition to a golf course architect, Mike loved the artistic component of the city. Heidi loved the beauty and history of downtown. To the little girls who were reared here, now 20-somethings Dana and Andrea, it was simply home. "There was never a reason to leave," says Heidi, simply. "At one point many years ago, Mike was thinking we should relocate back to Toledo. Then we were visiting at

Christmas and it was subzero. We needed a blowtorch to unfreeze the pipes. We got off the plane when we came home, and Mike went running that afternoon in 65-degree weather. The prospect of going back there permanently never came up again!"

It's a question that comes up whenever the subject of tongue cancer comes up. "Mike never dipped snuff," says Heidi, with a frustrated shake of the head. "He never chewed tobacco or smoked. Unfortunately, you are your genes, and there was cancer at an early age on both sides of Mike's family." Again she references the "old man's disease," versus more common (and more treatable, if discovered early) cancers like colon or prostate, which sometimes manifest in a man's late 40's or 50's. But while tongue cancer most often hits smokers and drinkers that are already old men, the cruel truth is that it's made Strantz, barely 50, one himself. The drawing that accompanies this profile was made from a photo taken prior to his health woes.

A writer once commented that Strantz, who loved to tour potential golf course sites on horseback, bore a strong resemblance to Wyatt Earp.

A writer once commented that Strantz, who loved to tour potential golf course sites on horseback, bore a strong resemblance to Wyatt Earp. But his towering frame is now stooped just a bit, his 60's-era hippie haircut, formerly scraggly and well below the shoulders, chopped much shorter. A bandana around the neck looks sporty, but is actually in place to mask a tracheotomy tube. About six months prior to moving into their new home, Mike underwent a full glossectomy. After removing all the tissue from his lower mouth, surgeons took portions of his scapula to reconstruct his jawbone, and muscle from one of his shoulders to reconstruct his tongue.

Despite his grave health, there are developers in the United States and abroad clamoring for his services, wanting an iconoclastic Strantz design sure to raise ire, admiration and undoubtedly attention. Well-known course architect Art Hills has known his fellow Toledo native for more than 20 years. "He's got so much talent, he's a wonderful artist, and is uniquely adept at putting that art on the ground. His courses are very artistic. Mike literally sketches the golf holes like a landscape artist before building them, and I know of nobody in the business who sketches as skillfully or accurately," concluded Hills, who's been in the business for 40 years.

For the time being, the former Architect of the Year, as named by *Golf World Magazine*, is on total sabbatical, taking on no work. He fulfilled his obligations on the West Coast, which were arranged prior to his debilitations. "Between designing and building the new house, moving in, our daughters and rigorous treatments to combat this aggressive cancer, that's more than enough for now," says Heidi, who gave up her career as a computer trainer to assist with her husband's health issues. "I can't even imagine trying to work at this point. Either of us," she says flatly.

Strantz is comfortable with the term "modern antiquities" in describing his courses. He agrees that many of them are more conducive to match play situations than the typical American emphasis on medal score.

Strantz is comfortable with the term "modern antiquities" in describing his courses. He agrees that many of them are more conducive to match play situations than the typical American emphasis on medal score. He writes, "They may not be 'fair,' at least from the perspective of typical resort or real estate development players."

What's left unsaid is that a traveling golfer, a discriminating student of the game who's experienced the great old courses of the British Isles and Ireland, "gets it." Those who have been lucky enough to experience firsthand the game in all its wild glory across the globe can appreciate the eccentricities, blind shots and extreme risk/reward elements this maverick (and principal of Maverick Course Design) puts into his work. He once said, "Some of the things we are doing today are tame in comparison to what was done at some of the great golf courses. If I built the Road Hole at St. Andrews today, people would say it was way too difficult. But that hole has been hailed over the years, so people don't have a problem with it. Time and tradition are great equalizers."

To date, the architect has only seven solo designs. Besides Bulls Bay, his best-known works are probably Caledonia Golf & Fish Club and True Blue Plantation, both on Pawleys Island near Myrtle Beach, and North Carolina's Tobacco Road and Tot Hill Farm. Questioned delicately about his legacy, his desire to further his mark in the field, the visions of holes, layouts and courses he has yet to realize, Strantz writes a simple answer on the whiteboard. "I would love to do more work. But I don't have much control over that. And I have to be satisfied with what I've done, which I am."

There might yet be outrageous designs he can transfer from his imagination to a green grass landscape. Someday he might confound or outrage his critics with a radical new design, intrigue a newcomer who quickly becomes a diehard proponent or expand his cult following. He looks out over the expansive marsh stretching endlessly beyond his showpiece home, perhaps contemplating this uncertain future. It's hard to say because the shadows fall across his ravaged face in the gathering dusk. Then he turns, and with a firm handshake, an appreciative nod and a warm smile, he soundlessly bids a visitor goodbye.

Author's Note: Mike succumbed to his illness less than two months after he and his wife, Heidi, welcomed me to their home to write this profile. I will always appreciate their willingness to entertain a stranger in such difficult circumstances.

On a recent summer afternoon in the gloaming, I experienced one of the proudest moments of what has been a mostly star-crossed life on the links. There have been plenty of fleeting highlights over the years - aces, eagles, rounds at or close to par, all of them of a personal nature. But this time, for the first time, it was a family affair.

Our youngest daughter, Kayla, has excelled at tennis during her middle school years, and very early in her tournament career her statewide ranking was within the top echelon. She's diminutive but competitive, and her trophy case is filled with the spoils of victory, often snatched from smug opponents, physically mature girls who tower over her childlike frame. We're understandably proud of her athletic achievements, but I always remind her that golf is exponentially more difficult than her sport of choice. Granted, the mental toughness required in a tennis match mirrors the psychological battles waged within oneself on a golf course. Stamina and fitness are mandatory on the courts also. But really, is there any comparison between knocking a fuzzy ball over a net with a large-headed racquet and attempting to maneuver a much smaller sphere into a gopher hole over acres and acres of turf, water, wetlands and sand? Nope, didn't think so.

Anyway, lately she's taken up a brief dalliance with golf. It's nothing serious, but a way to spend a bit of time with her old man, get a chance to steer the golf cart, kill an hour or so in the droning days of a seemingly endless summer vacation. Like any neophyte, the poor shots occur at double the rate of the good ones, but her progress has been tangible. Swinging and missing from the tee box has dwindled appreciably, and her touch around the greens, which not long ago was no better than that of a Bulgarian stonemason, has improved dramatically. But a steady diet of 8s, 9s and "others" in our truncated rounds shows she has miles, indeed light years, to go before reaching even a modest degree of proficiency. Nevertheless, not too long ago she showed a tantalizing glimpse of what might be.

The 16th hole at our home course is a short par 3. Perhaps 125 yards over a lagoon ringed with cattails and marsh grasses. The ladies tee is 20 yards closer still, and angled in a way that only a serious mis-hit will find the water. While I was fumbling with the clubs, Kayla, eschewing her normal routine of three or more practice swings, smote her kiddie driver a distance of exactly 100 yards. It arced onto the putting surface and rolled to the back tier, coming to rest perhaps 20 feet right of the hole, pin high. Needless to say, we were both ecstatic.

While her enthusiasm was unbridled, mine was tempered by the memory of a thousand similar moments of triumph immediately succeeded by some sort of disappointment. She scampered to the green and I was quick to follow, hoping to staunch the adrenaline flow, help her read the line - in short, do whatever possible to insure she didn't three-jack away her chance for her first indelible golf memory. To make a long story short, she rolled that sucker into the back of the cup, perfect speed. A deuce. We high-fived, hugged, and I told her one of the game's great and seldom-said truisms. "There's only one score you can make that's better than a two!"

This is a child who rarely makes a genuine double bogey, who's awaiting her first legitimate bogey, never mind a par, never mind a birdie. But two exquisite shots in succession gave her an ephemeral but tantalizing look at the game's appeal. Now she'll always know what the rest of us know. We suffer through the slices and chili-dips, we slog on through rounds where our chance to stay below triple digits ends with a pair of water balls on the penultimate hole. We go bunker to bunker, and then three-putt once we're finally on the green. We put up with all the middling play we subject ourselves to because you never know what type of magic is waiting on the next tee box.

Never mind a golf memory she'll cherish for a lifetime, look at the psychological weapon she's put in my arsenal! Next time she would rather stare vapidly at the television or bang the tennis ball against the garage, I know just how to wheedle her onto the course. "Come on, Kayla! You're due for another birdie!" A tiny seed has been planted. Let's see if the golf obsession grows.

PROFILE: LEA ANNE BROWN

It wasn't the easiest way to begin a birthday. At the tail end of a long, hard-partying Halloween weekend, a predawn wakeup call was followed by three hours in the car. But things took a most delightful turn several hours after sunrise. It's hard to say what the most attractive component of the morning's first appointment might have been. The day was sparkling, as pretty as a still-life painting. Bulls Bay is a good-looking track to begin with and among the most distinctively original properties in greater Charleston. Lea Anne Brown was my esteemed golf companion, every bit the equal of the weather and venue. There's no need to rank, file or categorize. It was a fortunate accident of fate to be in the middle of such a wonderful Triple Crown.

"I don't know where I'd be without golf," admits Lea Anne in mid round. Perhaps not far from her ancestral home of Owenton, Kentucky, she theorizes, not much more than a wide spot in the road south of Cincinnati and east of Louisville. But there were a pair of courses in this hamlet of 1,400, and her chiropractor parents would bring their little daughter, her twin brother, Matthew, and their older sibling, Mark, to the on-course nursery. It was only a matter of time before she joined the family fun. She shed 20-odd shots from the scorecard in a couple of year's time as a teen, her game evolving to the point that the University of Kentucky came calling for Miss Lea Anne Toftness. Things moved quickly in the early 80's. First was a college graduation in '82, a marriage to golf professional Hart Brown in '83 and a move to Charleston in '84 where he found work at Kiawah.

Lea Anne made her presence felt early and often on the city golf scene. Blonde, blue-eyed and with a bright smile, she looks like a Madonna but eventually seemed like a Medusa to the poor cadre of accomplished women players who vied for the major titles before the Browns descended southward after a brief dalliance in Charlotte. She won the women's division of the Charleston City Amateur Championship nine times consecutively from '84 to '92. A loss in '93 was avenged in '94. She took a decade off then won it again. She explains her long hiatus. "I didn't feel like I had anything left to prove," she says with a smile, not a hint of attitude. In '05, she was even more dominant than usual, winning the stroke-play portion of the event by 15 shots.

Although who would begrudge her a tinge of 'tude, considering her dominance has extended well beyond the city limits. She and her partner, Bubba Hightower, captured the State Mixed Team Championship in '04. She won the stroke play portion of the South Carolina Women's Amateur in '91 and '03, and the match-play portion of the event in '91, '92 and '93. Winning both disciplines of the state's premier women's amateur event in the same year as she did in '91 has only been accomplished by one other woman.

> *"I don't know where I'd be without golf," admits Lea Anne in mid round.*

Luckily her place in South Carolina's rich golf history is secure, because there was a rude awakening in the match-play finals of '04. The normally unsinkable Ms. Brown was undone by a precocious 13-year-old more than 30 years her junior. "It was a shock," admits Lea Anne, who had reeled off almost all of her city championships before the youthful interloper was even born.

Her husband Hart has almost 20 years of tenure at the Country Club of Charleston. The head professional has presumably had dozens if not hundreds of students who require more attention than his wife because her swing action is simple and efficient. Compact might be the operative word. Lea Anne herself is compact, of average height and athletic build. Her swing is compact and her repeating action and accuracy condenses the golf course down to tee box, fairway and green. Her golf game isn't flashy, but relentlessly effective. Ninety-five out of every hundred handicap players would be well served in trading their game for hers. The others? Two might be legitimately better, the other three probably wouldn't be willing to give up the ability to hammer it 280 off the tee.

"I didn't feel like I had anything left to prove," she says, smiling, not a hint of attitude.

Lea Anne describes her game as "traditional," something of a throwback. She plays matter-of-factly, with few fireworks. Her modus operandi has always been to par her opponents to death, but once in a great while she'll unleash birdies like hailstones. "I was at a course in Myrtle Beach I'd never seen before," she recounts with a smile. "I made eight birdies. I had never made more than five, and I was telling the gals I was with to get me off the course before I broke a leg or hurt myself somehow."

The long gap in her competitive resume is mostly due to the fact that her job as head buyer at Wild Dunes kept her away from the golf course. There was a four-year fallow period where she barely touched a club at all, proving one of the great golf axioms that comes as such a shocker to every beginning bag boy or bottom-rung assistant pro: Being in the golf business can seriously impinge your ability to get on the course. Unless you land the right job. As a golf writer, for instance, or membership director at an up-and-coming club like Bulls Bay. "I began as a shop assistant at Seabrook Island when we first moved to town," she says, "then spent 14 great years in my position at Wild Dunes, working for Terry Florence. When Terry became director of golf at Bulls Bay, he recruited me over. He told me part of my duties would be playing golf with prospective members, and I couldn't believe it. I was so thrilled."

"It wasn't a hard decision to try and lure 'the queen of golf' from Seabrook to Wild Dunes," says her longtime boss, chuckling. "And it was an equally simple decision to try and get her to come over here. Lea Anne's just a wonderful person with a great work ethic. Never mind her purchasing acumen, which was one of the main reasons we won numerous merchandising and retail awards for our golf shops at Wild Dunes. But she can just light up a room and has tremendous interpersonal skills."

Lea Anne describes her game as "traditional," something of a throwback. She plays matter-of-factly, with few fireworks.

Loyalty is important to Lea Anne, but the prospect of building a membership from the ground up and maintaining her long-standing relationship with Terry won the day. "It was a tough decision for her to leave Wild Dunes, but we knew that her personality and charm were ideal for the job of membership director," continues Terry, a Charleston golf fixture for more than three decades. "The work ethic was important also, as she was starting basically from scratch. Not only has she attracted members, but she continues to make current members feel comfortable and at home here at Bulls Bay, which is part of our larger philosophy to begin with."

Lea Anne obviously excels at her work, despite the fact that her game must intimidate some prospects. During her tenure, membership has grown from less than 20 to some 250. She estimates there have been a minimum of 50 rounds played in the company of prospects, several of whom were taken aback at the thought of a woman joining them on the tee. Of course any resistance or patronization is usually quelled after the first seamless par, more often than not on the opening hole. "I suppose I've shot a better score than the potential club member 45 times out of 50," she says with a slight shrug. It's technically a sales job, but she's quick to admit there's not too much selling involved. "Bulls Bay sells itself. We have such a unique product, and it's a fun and friendly place to be. It's a relaxed atmosphere and an awesome golf course. The truth is we've attracted a good number of members from Wild Dunes, which is just 20 minutes away. Terry and I knew tons of members from our many years there, and have stayed in touch. The other thing is that they're attracted to our pace of play. There's very little pressure on the golf course here, we only average about 30 rounds a day."

Lea Anne obviously excels at her work, despite the fact that her game must intimidate some prospects. During her tenure, membership has grown from less than 20 to some 250.

She's truly come to consider Charleston home, citing the people, the food, the courses and the warmth of the local golf community in which she and her husband are so entrenched. "Once you're part of the golf life here, you quickly meet players from around the city, are welcome at other clubs, and have a real connection to so many wonderful individuals you might never have encountered otherwise," she says. "It's pretty special."

Lea Anne moonlights just a bit as an antique dealer. A friend brought her into the business years ago but eventually left the area, so she now flies solo. It's an interesting notion to consider her hunting around at yard sales or attending the occasional auction looking to unearth a treasure or two for her antique shop, because the proprietress herself is a rare and valuable commodity. She's one half of the city's best-known golf "power couple," and among the most celebrated and accomplished women players in recent Charleston history. The title of this book generally refers to the area's great venues, but nobody who's had the opportunity to watch her play the game or spend a bit of time in her easy company would dispute the following perception: Lea Anne Brown is undoubtedly one of the real golf charms of Charleston in her own right.

She's truly come to consider Charleston home, citing the people, the food, the courses and the warmth of the local golf community in which she and her husband are so entrenched.

Cherokee Plantation

YEMASSEE, SOUTH CAROLINA

Number 11, Par 3

*I*t makes perfect sense that the Charleston area has so many exclusive golf clubs. The city's deep roots, deep pockets and deep love of outdoor recreation make it something of a hotbed of high-end facilities. There's hush-hush Yeamans Hall Club, with its varied membership classifications. There's old guard Country Club of Charleston, where your grandmother's mother might have been a charter member. One can't disregard the ritzy Kiawah Island Club, with its two distinct course offerings. There's posh Briar's Creek on Johns Island, strategically located between the executive airport and the multimillion-dollar mansions on Kiawah. Bulls Bay is avant-garde in both design and membership philosophy. And while each of these facilities is wonderful in its own way, the simple truth is this: There is nothing remotely like Cherokee Plantation.

There is nothing remotely like Cherokee Plantation.

About an hour southwest of town lies not only the most exclusive club in greater Charleston, but truly one of the most exclusive clubs in the world. No need for hyperbole, as simple numbers tell the story. Consider this fast fact, summed up succinctly: 8,000 acres and less than 20 members.

The Cherokee concept of fractional plantation ownership is unique and worthy of a quick explanation. Pretend for a moment you're rich. Not run-of-the-mill wealthy. Not simply well-off or well-heeled, not just prosperous or comfortable, but affluent with a capital "A," a business mega-titan, or an inheritor of vast sums. Now say you also harbor a secret desire to be Lord of the Manner. Perhaps Master of the Hounds, Peer of the Realm, King of the Castle, Prince of the Plantation. But you're unwilling to underwrite the tremendous upkeep of a plantation by your lonesome. By joining Cherokee (current initiation is in the low seven figures) and contributing your portion of the annual upkeep (currently in the low six figures) a sportsman can enjoy the lush life - hunting, shooting, fishing, boating, horseback riding, spa treatments, family get-togethers, business entertaining, fine food, finer wines, plush accommodations, minute attention to detail by a dedicated staff, etc., at a fraction of what it would cost to finance the operation on an individual basis. Never mind Louisiana's claim. With seven miles of river frontage on the winding Combahee, natural wood duck habitats and some of the best quail hunting in the South, Cherokee is truly a Sportsman's Paradise.

Lest we forget, there's also an extremely underrated golf course on the property. This low-profile Donald Steel design is laid out on some 200 acres, which is less than 3 percent of the property in total. This land-use ratio is instructive. The golf scene is certainly more that 3 percent of Cherokee's appeal, but the game is not the raison d'etre by any means. Many of the members are in violation of the "14-club rule." (No, not the rule about the number of clubs allowed in the bag, but the tongue-in-cheek rule referring to the number of private clubs a person belongs to. Again, remember the demographic.) With memberships at places like Pine Valley, Shinnecock Hills, Deepdale and dozens of other world-class clubs at their disposal, the typical Cherokee member might well relegate golf to a secondary activity while in residence. They want to put birdies on the card, certainly, but are more concerned with wood duck, dove, quail and whatever other game bird might come into focus at the end of their gun barrels. To each his own, but there are thrills aplenty taking aim solely at the bamboo (grown on the property) flagsticks on each of the eccentrically wonderful 18 greens.

Architect Steel is an Englishman, and brings a links sensibility to this serene parkland setting, a playing field dotted with some of the most astonishingly dra-

matic live oak specimens this vagabond golfer has ever had the privilege to see. The links analogy is valid because the ground game is paramount here. The greens are mostly open in front and are accessible via the ground as well as the air. Bunkers are notable both because of their style and infrequency. Only 35 sand pits exist on the course, the vast majority greenside. They are sod-wall bunkers - easy to tumble into, harder to exit. The shallow, kidney-shaped sand hazard usually found in these parts doesn't exist at Cherokee.

The greens have slopes, slants and pitches that will challenge one's equilibrium as much as the putting stroke. The swales and hollows surrounding these pristine surfaces pitch and heave profoundly. The ground effects in combination with the mowing patterns are almost jarring in some cases. Some of the more memorable green complexes look like grassy Salvador Dali paintings, or giant-size strips of ribbon candy. The recovery options are many. A player can pitch, chip, flop, nip, bump, putt or bounce the golf ball onto the surface after missing the green. The recovery shots, and judging the putting line afterwards, are the essence of this wonderful course.

Fortyish Mark Tomedolskey is the Maytag repairman of Charleston-area golf pros. The director of golf oversees a facility that sees a per-day average of four players.

The outward nine is a beautiful farmland setting, with horses and rail fences setting the stage. This part of the layout is a delightful antiquity, the course seems culled from a distant era, with tee boxes just steps from the previous green. The second nine has a different sensibility. A large cypress swamp bisects the playing corridors, necessitating a couple of shuttle rides between greens and tees for the walking contingent. By further contrast, this inward nine is forested with hardwoods bracketing the line of play in a manner not seen previously. The second nine features three par 3's, par 4's and par 5's, which affords greater variety and scoring opportunities than the front.

Fortyish Mark Tomedolskey is the Maytag repairman of Charleston-area golf pros. The director of golf oversees a facility that sees a per-day average of four players. "The driver is available for use on practically every hole - it's very fair," contends this accomplished player, who's held the pro's position since opening day in 1999. "There's room off the tee, and things narrow as you head to the green. The precision is more on the approach shot, getting to the right section of the green, than it is on the tee shot."

A busy day at Cherokee is three groups, and a mad rush like that only comes about in season, between October and May. When the weather truly warms, there's almost no play whatsoever. A snapshot: In ten years spent at a North Carolina club prior to his Cherokee tenure, Tomedolskey found time to play in only one Carolinas section PGA event. Now he has the opportunity to play in four or five annually. Being tournament-tested on a regular basis has made him one of the finer players in the entire region.

"I do whatever is necessary around here," says the pro. "I'll handpick the range, wash golf carts, give extensive playing lessons to owners and their guests when they're on the property, do a bit of everything." He also handles transportation issues, works in marketing, and wears whatever hats are necessary to keep things running smoothly when golfers are ready to test their mettle on these meticulous fairways.

For those incredulous readers used to five-hour rounds and tee-time lotteries, who might be having a hard time digesting these facts, here's another. The new superintendent was onboard for three full weeks before he saw an honest-to-goodness golfer. No, he didn't start work during the Christmas holidays, or over Fourth of July weekend when it might've been hot as fireworks. He began working in "high season," September.

Critics and pundits often rush to judgment, affixing an early label that ultimately might be inaccurate or unfair. Early on, before Cherokee's signature greens were softened with aeration, before the encroaching fescues were cut back from the playing corridors, the course was dismissed by some so-called experts as tricked-up and unfair. This isn't the case. It's a very pleasing minimalist design, less dynamic than it is organic. It was made by Steel but sits softly on the landscape, nonetheless, and is a fine and fair test of the game.

If you have the right directions, this happy hunting ground, this summer camp for the superrich, is just a few miles off the interstate. But approaching from the main conduit between Savannah and Charleston, one must negotiate mile after mile of country road to find the entrance. It doesn't much matter how you get there, if you use the major artery of I-95 or the detour off the "Road to Nowhere." Choose whatever method you'd like to arrive at Cherokee, but also know this: If you're lucky enough to find yourself at Cherokee Plantation, you know you've truly arrived.

Number 15, Par 3

One of the great things about golf is that it's an empirical endeavor. Everything can be measured: the length of a course, the length of a tee shot, handicap, slope rating, the score recorded and the number of tournament victories. It's a game that lends itself to numbers. Though there have been a number of greatly skilled players that were born, raised, spent time or currently live in Charleston, just like a tournament scorecard that has been signed and attested, here's a fact beyond dispute. The finest and most accomplished golfer in the city's long history is Beth Daniel.

The numbers and accolades speak for themselves. She's a two-time U.S. Amateur Champion. She's recorded 33 official LPGA Tour victories thus far in a pro career now more than 25 years old, including a Major at the LPGA Championship. On 10 different occasions, Daniel has represented her country internationally as a member of the Curtis Cup, Solheim Cup and World Cup teams. As a professional, she was lauded as Rookie of the Year in '79, was named Player of the Year the following season, and took home the same award twice more after that. She's amassed well over $8 million in career earnings, earned a berth in the LPGA Hall of Fame in 1999, and was inducted into the World Golf Hall of Fame the year after.

"I was a teenage member of the Country Club of Charleston when I first met Beth," recalls Tommy Cuthbert, one of the region's most enduring and beloved golf personalities. "I was playing in junior championships, and she was just a little girl, following her parents around, chipping and putting. She's about eight years younger than I, and I actually knew her older brother Tony much better." Cuthbert has spent the bulk of his professional career on Kiawah Island, where he was the resort's longtime director of golf. But he was an assistant pro at the Country Club when Beth burst onto the national scene in 1975.

"She was working hard on her game as she entered her teenage years, and was very astute. You could also tell she loved what she was doing, all the practice and repetition. When she won the U.S. Amateur in her first appearance, the entire club was excited and delighted for her, and also a bit surprised." It wasn't her talent that was in doubt, but the wherewithal to maintain composure in pursuit of a national title. "When she won the Amateur again two years later, I could see she was going to be a real force in professional golf," adds Cuthbert, a former South Carolina Open champion. "She was very competitive, with a real killer instinct. From that point on, nothing she did surprised me. In a way, I'm surprised she didn't win more."

In a town where some folks think you're not a native unless your grandmother's grandmother was born within the city limits, the Daniel clan might be considered carpetbaggers. Her mom, Lucia, was born in town, but her dad, Bob, hailed from Greenville, in the upstate region of South Carolina. He headed south for schooling at The Citadel. Bob began as an accountant at the local Coca-Cola bottling plant, worked his way up and eventually became president. Beth was the youngest of the three children, following Tony and Tricia into the world and eventually to the Country Club of Charleston. Her brother was an accomplished junior player, and eventually a leader on The Citadel golf team. But that didn't stop his littlest sister from trying to keep up.

"I've known Beth for 40-odd years," explains Frank Ford III, another of Charleston's best-known golf names. "We're still very close friends, as close as you can be, really, considering she now lives more than 500 miles away. We've played plenty of golf together over the years, and she's a wonderful woman. She's also one of the most competitive people I've ever met," says Ford, who admits it takes one to know one.

"She built herself a gorgeous golf swing," he continues with admiration. "It's a swing that anyone would be well served to copy. When she was at her peak, she could play from tee to green as well as any golfer, male or female, I'd ever been around. It wouldn't surprise me if she won again on the ladies Tour."

ABC's golf commentator Judy Rankin, a fellow inductee in the LPGA Hall of Fame, is another Daniel devotee. "I've always thought Beth had one of the best if not *the* best golf swing since Mickey Wright," says Rankin, referring to the legendary LPGA star who amassed eight Major championships among her 82 official victories and was named Female Golfer of the Century by the Associated Press. "It's still one of the three or four best swings I've ever seen."

"I started playing when I was 6," reminisces Daniel. "I played in my first tournament at age 8, organized by Al Esposito, the Country Club of Charleston head pro who was wonderfully encouraging to me and all the juniors. When I was 10, I was playing around the state. I had some success at that level, but I was no Tiger Woods," she adds wryly. "At 16, I began playing nationally. I didn't do real well, but got valuable experience and got over the intimidation factor, which is a major hurdle when you're playing USGA events. One of the big turning points was when I played in an event and broke par three days in succession. It showed me I was capable of playing real tournament golf. I contacted some colleges, looking for scholarships." There was no recruiting war for the services of the gifted teenage golfer. "I was writing letters and begging," she explains with a chuckle.

Though there was no scholarship forthcoming, Daniel ended up at Furman. Part of her decision was because the school was in state, and she had an aunt and uncle who lived near the campus. There was no indication when she headed upstate to Greenville that the team she would soon join would be one of the most powerful in NCAA history and win the 1976 AIAW national championship. Her collegiate

colleagues included Betsy King, who eventually preceded her into the LPGA Hall of Fame by four years. She also played with Cindy Ferro, Beth Solomon and Sherri Turner, all of whom ultimately logged some time on the LPGA Tour. "None of us were really known on a national level when we came to school, but we all ended up with nice careers," she adds with typical understatement.

Trying to rank victories in terms of importance is tricky business, but after careful consideration, Daniel names her first U.S. Amateur win in '75 as the milestone moment. "That was the first Amateur I ever played in, and it truly kick-started the rest of my life in golf. It wasn't until I won that event that I started thinking I might be able to play the Tour. I was 18 when I broke through, and it opened my eyes as to the future possibilities. Until then I was planning on a career in sports administration and coaching. I had no Tour aspirations whatsoever. But needless to say, it opened up many doors for me."

The golfer is quick to point out her triumph in the 1990 LPGA Championship as another bellwether. "It's my only Major win, so obviously it's very important. I generally played well in Majors (30 other Top 10's through the 2004 season, including half a dozen runner-up finishes). On that same subject, it kind of bothers me that I didn't win a couple more, but Majors are generally won by players who are quite straight off the tee and putt very well. The two suspect parts of my game are driving accuracy and putting. I've always been long off the tee, but not always straight. My putting has been streaky my entire career, I'm not what you would deem a great putter. To get those two elements melding together those four particular weeks of the year is a difficult thing."

Other huge wins include her second U.S. Amateur in '77, her inaugural Tour win in '79, when she overcame rotten weather conditions and managed to sleep on the lead throughout, and her most recent triumph. Winning the Canadian Open in 2003 ended an eight-year drought, and made her the oldest player (46 years, 8 months at the time) to win a tournament on the LPGA Tour. "I prefer the way our former commissioner Ty Votaw refers to it," she says, smiling. "He calls me the most experienced player to win in Tour history."

Daniel has undergone droughts in the past, owing in part to her streaky putter. But a couple of two- or three-year winless streaks must've seemed like a radar blip compared to the eight-year hiatus she endured from '95 to '03. "I'm not someone who gives up easily. I've had plenty of injuries over the years that have slowed me down, but I've always tried to fight through them." A lower-back injury not only kept her out of action for months in the mid-80's, but forced her to adjust and learn to play with back pain. Several years later, mononucleosis derailed her for most of a season, and in the mid-90's a shoulder surgery relegated her to a cameo on the Tour where she has so often starred. She only appeared in nine events that year, while she normally averages almost three times as many a season.

Before she was a Tour star, she was a basketball stalwart, and before that a tagalong little sister to Tony and Tricia, scraping to keep up with her siblings. "Everyone knows Beth as this tall, regal athlete. But this competitive streak was showing when she was just a shrimp, a tiny kid trying to dig it out of the dirt and hold her own against the older kids," recalls Ford, about five years Daniel's senior and who preceded her as a Furman University golfer of note. In the formative years, long before the cameras arrived, she developed her intensity, the emotions-on-the-sleeve component that made her a firebrand on a circuit where smiling Nancy Lopez was the "It" girl, a prom queen in soft spikes, all smiles and waves.

Before she was a Tour star, she was a basketball stalwart, and before that a tagalong little sister to Tony and Tricia, scraping to keep up with her siblings.

"I beat clubs sometimes," admits Daniel. "I would get visibly angry when I hit a poor shot. This was when women golfers didn't really show their emotions. It's ironic, because nowadays it's okay, even encouraged. If I didn't like a shot I hit, I'd slam my club down and get it out of my system. The media at the time made it a bigger deal than it really was, in my opinion."

Close observers say Daniel's switch to a long putter led her back to the winner's circle, and her current record as the LPGA's oldest tournament winner. "It no secret I've had my share of putting problems," she acknowledges. Her first event with the broomstick also included a failsafe. "Eventually my teacher Mike McGetrick convinced me to use it in competition, back in 2000. I remember my first event. I took the 3-iron out of my bag instead of my regular putter. I left the short putter in there also, just in case things went haywire with the long putter." She putted well enough over the course of the four-day tournament to put the long iron back in the bag the very next week. The short putter was banished, and she has since become an official broomstick convert.

The career will end soon enough, the next chapter of Daniel's life as yet unplanned. "I think I can win again, otherwise I wouldn't be out here anymore. That said, I'm ready to walk away when the time comes, and not be emotional when doing so, which is a first for me. But for right now, I think I'm still competitive, so why leave just yet? I'll limit my schedule a bit, but still go out there 15 times or so."

Her on-course success will allow her the latitude to go and be and do whatever she'd like when she slips out of soft spikes for the last time as a tournament competitor. "I'm truly not sure what's coming next for me," she confesses. "I feel as though that will become clearer when I definitely decide to give up the Tour life." She's comfortable in South Florida, and a permanent return to the Carolina Lowcountry seems like a remote possibility, although one never knows. After all, it's been more than 30 years since Daniel first left Charleston to chase the ball down the fairway, and chase the fame and fortune that have been byproducts of her unique talent and intense determination. "I have many friends in Florida and a wonderful home. Life is good for me here."

Part of the appeal is the similarity between her adopted hometown of Delray Beach and her ancestral home. Unlike so much of strip mall Florida, Daniel lives in a community with an intimate downtown and a colorful history. Like her hometown, tourists and locals meld together into the fabric of daily life. She revels in the fact that, unlike in her hometown, she can walk the streets of Delray with the type of anonymity she forfeited when she became a golf celebrity some three decades past.

"Charleston will always be home," concludes the Hall of Famer, who has also been honored as one of the top-50 players in LPGA Tour history. "I miss the marshes, the incredibly golden Lowcountry vistas. I'm in close contact with my family and we spend time together both here and there. But the scenery and the feeling of the area is something I'll always love." Never in all her far-flung travels has she heard a negative word about the city of her birth - everyone loves Charleston. She remains proud of her roots in the city, and the citizenry of the region are equally proud of their most esteemed and accomplished professional golfer.

"Charleston will always be home," concludes the Hall of Famer, who has also been honored as one of the top-50 players in LPGA Tour history.

The Country Club of Charleston

CHARLESTON, SOUTH CAROLINA

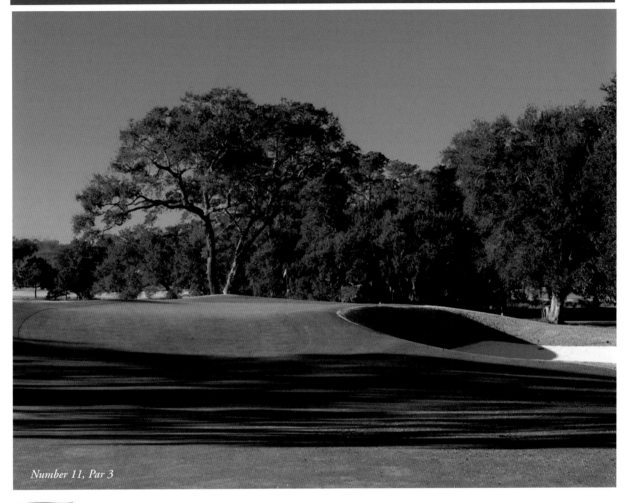

Number 11, Par 3

The Country Club of Charleston has many points of distinction, its wonderfully convenient location chief among them. There is no course in closer proximity to the downtown peninsula, and this anachronistic Seth Raynor gem is tucked just a minute or two off busy Folly Beach Road, perhaps a 10-minute drive from downtown.

The cover of this book depicts a golf scene at Harleston's Green, which was a predecessor of this, the city's oldest golf club. The earliest roots of the club date back to the 1780's, the Country Club was so named in 1901 and landscape engineer Raynor delivered the present routing in 1925. Previously a town surveyor used to working in straight lines, Raynor was a protégé of Charles Blair Macdonald,

one of the leading lights of golf architecture's so-called "Golden Age" of the 1920's. Macdonald and Raynor created courses in the era of Donald Ross, A.W. Tillinghast and Alister MacKenzie, among others. Much of the work of these masters has the enduring quality, classic strategy and timeless appeal sorely missing in the modern age of course design. Far too many signature courses are little more than a scrawl these days, with contrived and unnatural features that seem to be concocted by designers with massive egos and even bigger bulldozers. By contrast, the Country Club of Charleston is low profile, both on and off the greensward.

This is an eminently walker-friendly, classic parkland golf course, emphasis on "land" more so than "park." The fairways are ultra-wide and welcoming, with tree cover mostly an incidental presence. This fact, as it is throughout much of the greater-Charleston golf scene, is due mainly to the wicked force of Hurricane Hugo, which denuded the Country Club's landscape to the tune of a thousand trees when it ripped through the area in 1989.

"Strange as it sounds, many of us considered that storm to be almost a blessing in disguise," explains longtime member David Humphreys, who first joined the club in the early 70's.

"Strange as it sounds, many of us considered that storm to be almost a blessing in disguise," explains longtime member David Humphreys, who first joined the club in the early 70's. "Even though we were closed down for a year, we chose to make some significant improvements during the rebuilding process. The course was tired. We rebuilt greens, did some bunker restoration, changed some tees around, added irrigation and generally enhanced the course. The consensus was that the course was far better a year after Hugo hit than it was the day before it struck."

The storm wreaked havoc with the tree canopy, but the low-profile bunkers were left intact. This game-board-flat property is rife with sand hazards, both fairway and greenside. The entry points are at ground level, while exiting normally requires a blast or a ball picked clean over a lip or grass mounding. Exiting a fairway bunker is little cause for concern, but greenside? That's a different story completely. A golfer long on course sense and short on accuracy might think carefully about laying up in front of a good percentage of the greens. Land short of the putting surface and more often than not you'll have a relatively straightforward chip. Take aim at the flag and drift in either direction, though, and the ball will carom hard off the steep banks bracketing most every putting surface, often coming to rest in the maw of these ubiquitous sand caverns. It'll be a long day on this short track, one that tops out at just below 6,600 yards from the tips. Most players don't have the talent and temperament to handle the 15- or 20-yard explosion shot, particularly when the ball must not only travel out, but also up above these steep-faced banks that are, on

some occasions, 10 or even 12 feet high.

Every spring, the club plays host to a gang that can handle the bunkers with aplomb, not to mention the slippery greens and strangling rough that are implemented for the occasion. The Azalea Invitational has been contested here since 1946, and some 60 years after Charleston golf legend Frank Ford Sr. won the inaugural event, the Azalea continues to attract one of the most stellar fields in amateur golf.

The roster of champions isn't riddled with golf celebrities, like many other prestigious amateur events of long duration. This is due to the fact that the tournament is always played in springtime. It's a rare occasion when the current collegiate crème de la crème can make their way to the event, busy as they are at the height of the college season. But make no mistake - there are very few amateur events that supersede the Azalea in terms of prestige, tradition, reputation and resume building. It mostly attracts the Mid-Am crowd, the 25 to 55 set, the career amateurs who play for the love of the game. And what's not to love when your skills are so developed, your reputation so well known that you're afforded a coveted invitation to play golf in one of the world's most desirable cities at the apex of her seasonal beauty? Indeed, there's much to love about a game that allows you to test wits, nerve and skill on a hard-running, shot-making, bunker-raking examination, with its linear angles, pushed-up "wedding cake" style greens, and sweeping city views.

The course abuts the Intracoastal Waterway as the inward journey begins. In spring and fall, the yachts, pleasure boats and cabin cruisers are making their way either to or from Florida. Time your appearance on the 10th tee just right, and it'll look as though one of these million-dollar vessels is plowing right across the fairway, such is the angle of the playing corridor and bend of the waterway.

The next hole is a conversation starter also, albeit for different reasons.

The next hole is a conversation starter also, albeit for different reasons. This 190-yard, redan-style par 3 has a green perched high in the air, flanked by twin bunkers that require a near vertical explosion shot to find purchase on the putting surface. Wait, there's more. The green has a pronounced slope, and the false front will repel any shot short of the surface perhaps 20 yards back down into the fairway. The upshot is that the hole was softened some years ago from even-more-exacting circumstances. Short of a palmetto tree directly in front of the tee box or a gremlin hired to yell "Boo!" in your backswing, it's hard to imagine what those circumstances entailed. Suffice it to say that, in days of yore, Slammin' Sammy Snead once carded an unlucky 13 on the hole. "It's a controversial hole, to say the least," offers George Bahto, author of "The Evangelist of Golf" and a noted Seth Raynor expert. "But I happen to like it because it's so different."

Number 12, Par 4

Far better is the staunch 16th, named "Lion's Mouth" because the massive circular bunker lazing before the putting surface is a dangerous predator. At 430 yards in length, popcorn hitters would be well served in laying up short in two, then either lofting a wedge over the abyss or skirting the danger with a bump-and-run. Anything to avoid the gut-checking alternative. "The 16th is the finest hole on the course," says Bahto. "The bunker pays homage to the fifth hole at St. Andrews and guards an excellent punch bowl green."

"It's clearly not that demanding off the tee," says Frank Ford III, longtime member, multiple club champion and six-time winner of the Azalea. "But when it's hard and fast, when the wind starts whipping and the greens firm up, it can be very tough. You need to position the ball properly on the fairway for

the best approach angle to the green. This is undoubtedly a second-shot course and a recovery course. To do well out here you need a solid iron game, be able to play in wind and have the ability to scramble for par from around the green, the bunkers in particular."

> *"To do well out here you need a solid iron game, be able to play in wind and have the ability to scramble for par from around the green, the bunkers in particular."*
> *– Frank Ford III*

Much like the recent renovations that have transpired at Yeamans Hall, the other Seth Raynor gem in town, there are also changes afoot at the Country Club. "It's been more than 15 years since the last significant modifications have been made," explains Tommy Ford, past president of the club and longtime board member. Tommy is Frank's uncle and multiple club champion and senior club champion in his own right. "We had some salt water issues on our greens some years back and we'll be resurfacing the greens at minimum. We're also inclined to redo some bunkers and tees and perhaps bring back some of the original Raynor sensibilities that have been lost over time."

Frank admits to bias, but considers his home course to be among the three best in the area, along with Yeamans Hall and the Ocean Course. "Any skill level can enjoy the Country Club. The weaker player can bounce and run the ball onto the greens, providing he can hit it straight enough. A more powerful player can land the ball squarely on the putting surface, but some of our pin positions make it extremely difficult to get the ball near the hole. It might be much shorter for the power player, but it can still be very difficult. I like the style of golf we have here, where you can play through the air or along the ground, depending on individual preference and the course or weather conditions."

The former golf administrator in both South Carolina and Georgia knows of what he speaks. Not only is the Country Club one of the region's oldest courses, it's also among the very best.

Contrary to what some observers might believe, Frank Ford III does not spend every waking moment on the golf course. It's just that his competitive record, longtime dominance of the Charleston golf scene, handicap index and legacy make it seem that way.

I know this to be true because Ford received me in his spacious Meeting Street office on a weekday afternoon, clad in dress shirt and tie, stock quotes flashing on his desktop computer terminal. His prodigious golf ability may assist him in his livelihood, but it isn't his means of support. He's been a financial advisor for more than two decades, and there are few fields of endeavor better suited for a scratch golfer to scratch out a nice living. It's a make-or-break world, and Ford must make quite the impression when he breaks par in the company of potential customers. If his client portfolio is as stuffed as his trophy case, then rest assured he's doing just fine.

Frank Ford III is a sixth-generation Charlestonian, which isn't all that impressive in a town that practically breathes its collective history.

Frank Ford III is a sixth-generation Charlestonian, which isn't all that impressive in a town that practically breathes its collective history. He is, however, a third-generation golf champion, and grandson of Frank Ford Sr., perhaps the most legendary local figure in the history of Charleston golf. "I remember the exact circumstances when granddad finally gave up the game," reminisces Ford with a chuckle. "We had just finished nine holes. He birdied the last for a score of 45. Someone complemented him on shooting halfway to his age, as he was 90 at the time. Of course, he had bettered his age hundreds of times in the past. But he thought for a second, realized 45 and 45 was 90, and quit on the spot. He wasn't going to be a 90's shooter, and he never went out again."

If that little anecdote provides a sliver of insight into the competitive psyche of Frank the First, consider this: When grandson won his third Azalea Invitational, one of the nation's premier amateur events, the then 84-year-old came onto the final green and said, "Congratulations, Bubba. And now you can stop right there." The old man had won four Azaleas, including the first two ever contested in the mid-40's, and wanted his record unchallenged. Think "Bubba" doesn't have the same competitive streak?

He went out and won three more in succession, and owns six titles to granddad's four. Of course, he only has one South Carolina Amateur title, and the old man won seven. On the other hand, Frank III won the even-more-prestigious Carolinas Amateur, a title his granddad never captured. And so on.

Missing in this mix is Frank Sr.'s firstborn son Frank Jr. September 11 is a date that has been burned into our collective psyche since the tragedies of 2001. But for the Ford family, it's been a milestone of grief for almost 30 years longer than that. Frank Jr. was only 44 when he perished in an airline crash on that date in 1974, and his son Frank III, a recent graduate and scholarship golfer at Furman University, was still in his early 20's. He was an important part of the family's building-supply business, the father of two other children besides Frank III, and a talented golfer by most any stretch of the imagination, a 2 or 3 handicapper. But all things are relative. He was a fine athlete but suffered with polio as a child. Compared to his father or his oldest son, Frank Jr. was good but not great, a solid player, but not of the same tournament caliber.

Frank Sr. initially learned of the game he'd come to dominate around Charleston early last century near his home in Summerville. His original instructors were caddies, at a little homemade course they had set up in the woods. These were the first folks who showed him how to hold a club and swing it properly. Though he had plenty of ability, this original golfing Ford never had professional aspirations. The height of his playing career coincided with the Depression, and it just wasn't meant to be. He did, however, influence the career of another well-known player of the era.

Frank Sr. was a contemporary of Henry Picard, the longtime Country Club of Charleston head professional. Seventy-odd years ago, Picard was thinking about taking a run at the pro touring circuit, but Frank Sr. urged caution. "How will you make it out there if you can't even beat me?" Is how Frank III relates the story. Picard retorted that if he could beat Frank Sr. three times in succession he'd have the confidence to attempt the touring life. Eventually he won the three matches, went out into the tournament world and took home a Masters jacket and a PGA Championship trophy for his trouble. And his benchmark for doing so was Frank Sr., the best player at the club where he was employed.

"I've known Frank III for well over 30 years," explains Kevin King of Hilton Head, another of South Carolina's more renowned amateur golfers. "We've played a ton of golf, both with and against each other. We've played in U.S. Amateurs, Mid-Amateurs, Palmetto Cups and other regional events. He's one of the most remarkable people I've ever met in the game. He's a purist, he knows the rules, and his family is probably the biggest golf family in the state's history. You have to mention the Haas family also, but the Fords have such longevity, beginning of course with Frank Sr. We've spent plenty of time off the course, traveling and whatnot. Frank III is just a high-quality guy in every way, and well worth knowing, on and off the course."

Anyone with a record as consistent and competitive as Ford's will always entertain the notion of taking it up to the next level, and approaching Champions Tour eligibility a few years back, Frank III was no exception. But shortly after his 50th birthday he was hit with a double whammy. First, numbness in his hand quickly led to neck surgery. An old football injury had deteriorated to the point that a disk needed to be fused. Shortly after recovery ensued, he was waylaid by a semi-serious auto accident that ruined the rest of what was left of the season. "The Champions Tour was in the back of my mind," says Ford, now in his mid-50's. "And that's exactly where it's going to stay!"

"The Champions Tour was in the back of my mind," says Ford, now in his mid-50's. "And that's exactly where it's going to stay!"

Frank III and his wife, Frances, have four children. This fourth generation of Ford golfers might be shaping up to be at least as skillful as the ones before. Their oldest son has a game that's as snappily efficient as his name. Cordes (rhymes with hoards - as in strokes) Ford is a youthful-looking, 30-something Charleston lawyer and father of two. (He's officially Frank IV, but is known by his middle name to minimize confusion.) He's also a former winner of the Carolinas Amateur and the current course record holder at Country Club of Charleston. Think about that one for a second. How many thousands of sterling under-par rounds have all these Fords forged over the years on their home track? Yet nobody, not his dad, the granddad he never knew, the great-granddad he knew well, his uncles, aunts, grandmother, etc., have ever made their way from first hole to last in as little as 62 blows, which is the number Cordes recorded in 1998. Although it's nigh impossible to discount them, look beyond the Fords, and consider all the great players in 75-plus years who've had a go at this historic track. Ben Hogan, Sam Snead and former head professional Henry Picard among others, winners of 18 major championships between them, not to mention 60 years worth of high-caliber amateur competition at the Azalea Invitational. Cordes' success as a fourth-generation champion further cements a truth that has been self-evident for decades: Like the Flying Wallendas to the high wire or the Corleone family to crime, so are the Fords to Charleston golf - an indomitable force.

Hart Brown has been the head professional at the Country Club of Charleston for some 20 years, and is well qualified to expound on the multi-generational talents of the Fords. "Frank Sr. is truly the patriarch of Charleston golf," explains the pro, who came on the scene when Frank the First was in his early 80's. "He really stood for honesty and integrity, and loved to see his many descendants learn and ultimately excel at golf. Tommy is Frank's youngest son, and an uncle to Frank III, although he's not even 10 years older than his nephew. He's the former president of our club, a wonderful golf photographer (whose work is found elsewhere in this book) and probably has the most technically sound golf swing of them all. His competitive record doesn't really reflect how good a player he is, though he's coming into his own as a senior player. Frank III is the most competitive of the Fords, and has the most involvement with the game, serving on USGA committees and such. I think his tournament record is the most impressive in the family, and supersedes his grandfather's. That's only my opinion, and there are others who feel the opposite. Cordes I've watched since he was just a kid. There were thoughts that he might turn professional, but after giving it his all one summer in amateur competition, he decided he couldn't quite make it to that next level."

While this Ford foursome is the competitive mainstay of the clan, various other family members have captured assorted championships over time. "There's no way to really explain it," concludes Brown, smiling. "It's just in their genes."

Frank III has likely been asked the question as often as he's signed a competition scorecard. How do you explain the Ford phenomenon?

Frank III has likely been asked the question as often as he's signed a competition scorecard. How do you explain the Ford phenomenon? He answers thoughtfully. "My granddad was a wonderful natural athlete and very competitive. He spawned a natural competitiveness within the family. He set a mark that was very high, and golf has just become a part of this family. There has been an expectation about the game that can be dangerous, or at least damaging. Some of us have lived up to it, and others have chosen to pursue other interests entirely. In the total scheme of things, golf isn't that important." Here he pauses for a moment, then adds with a wink, "Unless you play."

Frank Sr. provided the golf impetus, and his progeny have followed his lead. "Even his mother, my great-grandmother, Sissie, eventually took up the game and won a club championship," continues Frank III. "All the boys played, my dad and two uncles, and they drove each other. My uncle Tommy has the best swing in the family, and has become a senior player of note. My uncle Billy was a wonderful junior and collegiate player, a contemporary of Arnold Palmer. He had pro-caliber talent but never pursued it to that level. My sister, Anne, has won city championships in Winston-Salem. My mother, Sarah, has been competitive at the state level and won numerous club championships. In fact, she won the women's club championship recently at age 71."

Frank III also has a brother named Tim who barely plays at all anymore, though his natural ability and solid swing would allow him to shoot in the 80's right from the get-go. His cousins play some, but not with any regularity or distinction. "The golf gene in our family seems to spread more vertically than horizontally," he offers with a chuckle. Cordes is the leading golf light in the fourth generation, his three siblings and various cousins aren't as interested in pursuing the game, at least not yet.

"My great-grandfather was competitive to the very end," adds Cordes. "Even though he gave up golf at 90, he continued to hunt for many years after. He always wanted to bag one more buck, but he started going less often, his eyesight started failing, and he couldn't get it done. Instead he turned his attention to living to 100. Sure enough, he made it, and he died just a couple of days after his 100th birthday in the summer of 2004."

Though his skill level is unquestioned, Cordes is still waiting for his first Country Club of Charleston club championship. He had a golden opportunity a short while ago, but the man who rocked his cradle wrecked his chances. "I was 1-up on my dad in the Match Play Championship semi-finals in 2003," recalls the slightly built attorney. "We were both under par and playing well. I hit a 9-iron to about five feet on the eighth hole and figured I'd extend my lead. Dad responded by holing a wedge shot for an eagle 2 and tying the match. He went on to beat me, and won another title." Perhaps Cordes will pull the same trick on Nathaniel in 20 or 30 years time. His toddling son (the first firstborn Ford not christened Francis Cordes Ford since the 19th century, by the way) is showing promise with his plastic clubs, and will soon graduate to metal kiddie clubs. "He's going at it one-handed for now," explains his dad, "but he'll get both hands on the grip before long."

Nathaniel is among the first generation of Fords who'll grow up without knowing "the old man," Frank Sr., his great-great-granddad ...

Nathaniel is among the first generation of Fords who'll grow up without knowing "the old man," Frank Sr., his great-great-granddad, who died when he was just a baby. But he'll be nurtured in the game by his dad and doting grandfather Frank III. His championship pedigree is unquestioned, but whether he's of championship stock himself is a question that won't be answered for many years. But the odds are good that he is, and the child might well carry on the Ford championship mantle, a legacy that has become both self-perpetuating and self-sustaining.

Tracking the Tournament Triumphs by Generations

The First Generation
Frank Ford Sr.
18 Country Club of Charleston Club Championships
11 Charleston City Championships
7 South Carolina Amateur Championships
4 Azalea Invitational Championships
Elected to the South Carolina Golf, Carolinas Golf and South Carolina Athletic Halls of Fame.

Note: His mother, sister and brother each won a Country Club of Charleston Club Championship.

Betsy Coker Ford (Wife of Frank Sr.)
6 Country Club of Charleston Women's Championships
2 Charleston City Women's Championships

The Second Generation
Thomas Ford
7 Country Club of Charleston Club Championships
3 Country Club of Charleston Senior Championships
4 Charleston City Senior Championships

William Ford
3 Country Club of Charleston Club Championships
Captain of the University of North Carolina Golf Team

Sarah Ford Rijswijk (Widow of Frank Ford Jr.)
6 Country Club of Charleston Women's Championships
1 Charleston City Championship

The Third Generation
Frank Ford III
16 Country Club of Charleston Club Championships
10-time U.S. Amateur participant
6 Charleston City Championships
6 Azalea Invitational Championships
1 South Carolina State Amateur
1 Carolinas Amateur
1 Carolinas Mid-Amateur
Member of the South Carolina Golf Hall of Fame

Anne Ford Strickland (Sister of Frank III)
7 Old Town Club Women's Championships
2 Winston-Salem City Championships

The Fourth Generation
Cordes Ford (Son of Frank III)
4 Country Club of Charleston Junior Championships
2 South Carolina Private School Championships
1 Charleston City Championship
1 Carolinas Amateur Championship
Country Club of Charleston Course Record Holder (62)

Beresford Creek

Number 17, Par 3

The operative word at Daniel Island is "roomy." This land mass is 4,000 acres in total, surrounded by 23 miles of rivers and creeks. There are only some 3,000 residents sharing the abundant acreage, replete with hundreds of acres of parks and a nature preserve to boot. An oasis of this caliber just 15 minutes from both downtown and the airport won't stay thinly settled for long, though. In a decade's time there might be as many as 15,000 residents, as the island is zoned for 7,000 private homes, townhomes and condos.

Chief among the myriad attractions at this unique island town are 36 holes of wonderful golf at the Daniel Island Club, courtesy of architectural icons Tom Fazio and Rees Jones. Fazio delivered Beresford Creek in 2000, and the Jones-designed Ralston Creek was unveiled six years later, in 2006. The growing membership may have been weaned on the single Fazio track for half a decade, but that was no great burden. The course is a keeper.

"Because Daniel Island is actually a part of the city itself, it was logical for me to produce a design like the in-town golf clubs of yesteryear," explains Fazio. "The parkland style was a natural for us. Even though there was dense vegetation on site, there was also lots of open space for us to work with. We used the open space, the massive trees and the wetlands to our advantage."

This parkland track offers the same sensibility as the island on which it exists - roomy. Stretching to 7,200 yards from the tips, most players will do fine from the

Number 2, Par 4 and Number 3, Par 5

blue markers, at 6,850 yards with a 135 slope rating. The white tees are a shade below 6,400 yards, sloped at 130. The course routing is a pair of clockwise loops, a simple and effective use of the land available. Playing corridors are wide, green complexes typically generous, trouble found mostly at the periphery. There are homes on the property, though at this juncture only in small clusters. But unlike many real estate golf developments, the structures at Daniel Island actually serve to enhance the playing experience, odd as that may sound. First of all, the homes are stately. Secondly, in almost every case the setbacks for the property are overly generous. Only the most egregiously misdirected golf ball will trickle into someone's yard. The elegant housing, viewed as it is from a distance, serves to underscore the classy and tasteful sensibility of the property as a whole.

This parkland track offers the same sensibility as the island on which it exists - roomy.

The Bermuda-grass greens at Daniel Island are among the fastest and truest in the city. There are chipping collars on many holes, allowing the majority of players who miss the green in regulation the option of putting, chipping, pitching or using a flop shot to advance the ball onto the surface.

The course is straightforward, everything out in front, with no hidden hazards. Only rarely must a hazard be negotiated from the tee, never from fairway to green. Fazio has employed some thoughtful cross-bunkering though, and water lurks on the periphery of certain holes. Here the challenge is not launching a ball over, but steering away from the ponds and lagoons dotting the property.

For a golf course constructed at sea level, Beresford Creek offers some unusual playing characteristics. The fairways have a bit of pitch and roll to them, and flat lies aren't necessarily a given. "We used the earth we had to dig for irrigation and drainage throughout the playing corridors of the golf course. It gave us some elevation and roll, which offer variety, framing and challenge," continues the architect.

Along the same lines, there are numerous plateau greens on the property. The architect created putting surfaces that rise above the fairway. The greens are open in front, and will accept a shot that runs up to the surface, assuming the ball has enough zip to actu-

ally scoot all the way to a flagstick perched well above the fairway. There are large fairway bunkers in play throughout the course. With flashed faces, expect these sand caverns to exact a real penalty on the scorecard. Only the skilled player will be able to meaningfully advance a ball that's resting at the bottom of one of these widely scattered bunker complexes.

For a golf course constructed at sea level, Beresford Creek offers some unusual playing characteristics. The fairways have a bit of pitch and roll to them, and flat lies aren't necessarily a given.

Midway through the inward nine, Route 526, which serves as Charleston's beltway loop, appears in the middle distance. Strangely enough, much like the graceful housing that serves as a counterpoint to the wide-open parkland style of the front nine, the bustling roadway offers a unique perspective to the quietude of the closing holes, surrounded as they are by acres of wetland and marsh. It serves as an unusual reminder that this lovely residential setting is well within the city limits, and though seemingly a world apart, offers extremely convenient access to the city proper. Whatever minimal distraction the highway provides, thankfully it abates in the nick of time, as the closing holes demand a golfer's full attention.

As the round winds down, the property constricts. Fairways tighten, approaches pinch in. The course really strengthens down the stretch. The 14th is a wonderful par 4 bisected by a massive oak tree with a green surrounded by marshland. The penultimate hole is the best par 3 on the course, 185 yards in length with a massive wetland sure to envelop any ball left of the target. The last is a brutish par 4, 450 yards from the blue markers, where a solid blow is required just to clear the wetlands and find short grass. From here, expect a 200-plus-yard approach to a tilting putting surface with water short left and bunkers right. Luckily, the clubhouse is nigh and the welcoming oak tavern offers respite from this daunting conclusion just a chip shot away. "The finishing holes meander through some of the great marshland on the western side of the property," concludes Fazio. "It makes for a challenging and beautiful finish."

Daniel Island offers a unique mode of club transport that this vagabond golfer had never previously encountered. It's a remote-controlled-caddie apparatus called a "Shedda." It looks like a grocery shopping cart that has been put in the trash compactor. Or maybe a mini Moon Rover, the type of toy an indulged child might receive as a gift, bought for a couple of grand in the catalog pages of Hammacher Schlemmer.

Whatever it looks like, this remarkable contraption, part caddie, part rolling beverage cart, follows its "master" silently down the fairway.

Whatever it looks like, this remarkable contraption, part caddie, part rolling beverage cart, follows its "master" silently down the fairway. When you take off down the fairway, it does too. When you stop, it stops. When you turn, it turns. It underscores the walking sensibility at the Daniel Island Club, where an admirable percentage of play is conducted by folks traversing the course under their own power. Some carry, others use pull carts, and some have gotten used to this newfangled and addictive mechanism. Whatever their pleasure, all the amblers are doing themselves and the course conditions a great service.

A brief word about the affability of the membership in closing. On an initial reconnaissance mission, I inadvertently strafed a trio of women leaving the seventh green. (Here's an excuse, somewhere on the spectrum between lame and legitimate: Recent heavy rains had made the normally firm and fast fairways wet to the point of saturation. The yardage markers on the sprinkler heads were mostly obscured under muddy water, so I had to eyeball the proper distances. Not only was the direction of my approach shot lacking, but as an added bonus, I was two clubs too strong. Of course, an extra 30 seconds of patience on my part would've rendered the point moot.)

Anyway, these ladies quickly waved me through (obviously thinking they were safer in arrears than ahead) and couldn't have been nicer about it. They were downright jovial, and why shouldn't they be? With a course as pleasant and pastoral as Beresford Creek at their disposal, and Ralston Creek certain to provide an equally agreeable test of the game, most anyone would be in a similarly fine humor.

Number 14, Par 4

ESSAY: ETIQUETTE COURT (A ONE ACT PLAY)

Most all golfers learn the rudiments of etiquette early on. You don't talk while someone else is playing a shot, don't stumble across your opponent's putting line, rake the bunkers, etc. But there are a variety of subtler issues also in play. Etiquette Court is now in session:

BAILIFF: All rise! Etiquette Court is now in session, the Honorable Phil Divitz presiding.

JUDGE: Be seated, and thank you bailiff. Tell me, what's on our agenda this morning?

BAILIFF: Our first case is Carl "the Commentator" Carmichael. His regular foursome accuses him of never letting a single shot he executes play out in silence. He somehow feels everyone wants to know his thought process on each of his 110 strokes.

JUDGE: What do you have to say for yourself, Carmichael?

CARMICHAEL: I dunno, Judge. It's a nervous habit, I guess.

Nobody, I mean no-body, cares that you "caught that one on the screws."

JUDGE: Mr. Carmichael, let me explain something. Nobody, I mean no-body, cares that you "caught that one on the screws," or that you were waffling between a 4- and 5-iron, that you thought the wind would carry your tee ball to the back shelf or that your putt stayed out because it hit a spike mark. Do you understand me? Good. As it's your first appearance in Etiquette Court, I'll let you off with a warning. Just don't let me see you in here again. Next case!

BAILIFF: This is a similar case, Judge. Otto "the Optimist" Owens is accused of prematurely exclaiming how everyone's shots are so wonderful, even though they usually aren't.

JUDGE: In here once again Otto, I see. You know how I abhor half-baked optimists on the golf course, don't you.

OWENS: Sorry, Judge. It's just that I want my playing companions to hit good shots all the time and I guess I get carried away.

JUDGE: Owens, to be frank, you are a dolt. At least the last guy is easy to tune out, because he just natters on incessantly about his own strategy and results. You are a more insidious case because your playing partners can't help but hold out hope you are speaking the truth about their mostly mediocre shots. I've said this before, and before I pass sentence I'll repeat myself. Not every drive is "center cut," as you so quickly exclaim when it's leaving the club-face. Not every approach is "right at the stick." Not every putt, as you so maddeningly insist, is "Draino!" You are a chronic cockeyed optimist, and you need to be taught a lesson. Thirty days on the tennis court. Next case!

BAILIFF: "Bluto" Bardwell has a reputation for never fixing a ball mark on the green.

JUDGE: Bardwell, I've never laid eyes on you before, but I detest those of your ilk.

BARDWELL: Judge, I've never been hunting in my life! I've never shot a deer, a rabbit or an ilk.

JUDGE: That's an elk, not an ilk, you nincompoop! Why don't you fix ball marks, you simpleton?

BARDWELL: Because I'm lazy?

Exactly, although "fat and lazy" is a more accurate description.

JUDGE: Exactly, although "fat and lazy" is a more accurate description. And besides that, you're inconsiderate, ill-mannered and selfish. Fixing a ball mark takes five seconds, but one that's not repaired takes weeks to heal. From now on, you will fix not only the ball marks you make, but an additional mark as well. Never let me see you in this courtroom again, Bardwell, or the consequences will be severe. Next case!

I'm not a big fan of selfish golfers, Feely. But I'll consider leniency in this case if you can answer a simple question. How much does a flagstick weigh?

BAILIFF: Our final case is brought against "Self-Absorbed" Stanley Feely. He's accused of general malaise by his foursome. He doesn't help look for lost balls, always grabs his putter and wedge and expects his cart partner to drive up to the green, things of that nature.

JUDGE: I'm not a big fan of selfish golfers, Feely.

But I'll consider leniency in this case if you can answer a simple question. How much does a flagstick weigh?

FEELY: I have no idea, Judge.

JUDGE: I bet you don't. That's because you've probably never picked one up and replaced it in the hole after everyone has putted out, isn't that so? Well if you think that's too much of a bother, try 60 days of yard work and cleaning the garage, which is the sentence I impose. When you get back on the golf course in a couple of months, assisting your mates will seem like a breeze in comparison, won't it? And now if you'll all excuse me, I have a tee time to get to myself. Court adjourned!

Ralston Creek

Number 3, Par 5

In addition to its lovely Lowcountry setting and thoughtful design characteristics, the Ralston Creek course at Daniel Island is a significant part of the Charleston golf landscape for an altogether different reason. It's the newest course in the region, officially opening for play in 2006. And with no major projects on the horizon in the foreseeable future, Ralston will be "the new kid in town" for at least a little while longer. Classic courses are great, and fit in especially well in a town with a history as long and rich as Charleston's. But there's also something to be said for the modern marvel, and Ralston Creek is just that.

"This is a wonderful setting I've been given to work with," begins course architect Rees Jones. "I've always thought that architecture improves considerably when the owner provides a quality piece of land, replete with great views, marshland and inherent drama. Ralston Creek has beautiful marsh-side holes and gorgeous live oaks framing the fairways."

"This is a wonderful setting I've been given to work with," begins course architect Rees Jones.

Jones is no stranger to the area, having previously designed The Golf Club at Briar's Creek. He says the variety of holes at Ralston Creek is one of the most notable aspects of the course. "It unfolds among the live oaks, then moves out to the marsh towards the

Number 9, Par 3

conclusion of the opening nine, returns inland for a bit, then returns to the marsh midway through the inward nine. The course finishes with a beautiful par 5 featuring a blend of water and sand hazards, as well as a green complex guarded by grandiose live oaks along the right, a strategic pond on the left and open marshland in the rear." Jones describes the ebb and flow of Ralston Creek: "We have wooded holes, holes that skirt the natural features and wetlands, holes that are fairly open and some that are narrow."

Jones admits that the eighth hole, a delicate dogleg-left over the marsh, is his homage to the penultimate hole at Maidstone.

The course dovetails nicely with the original Tom Fazio effort from 2000, and it's gratifying that both golf experiences are eminently walker friendly. The first tees of each course are in fairly close proximity, and both layouts conclude near the clubhouse. To maximize the unique site attributes and develop a diverse and memorable golf experience, the Ralston Course was conceived as a "continuous 18" routing, with the breathtaking ninth hole situated on the northernmost point of the island. Like its predecessor, the first segment of Ralston Creek is parkland style. But long marsh views change the sensibility in mid round, particularly on holes eight, nine and 10.

Jones admits that the eighth hole, a delicate dogleg-left over the marsh, is his homage to the penultimate hole at Maidstone. This 1891 classic on eastern Long Island is a longtime favorite of the architect. Challenge the brunt of the marsh from the tee and be rewarded with a shorter iron home. But a conservative play to the right to avoid the marsh might well result in a drive that finds the sand on the outside of the dogleg, as a row of target bunkers are the aiming point from the tee. "You can bite off as much as you can chew, though it doesn't necessarily make sense to cut the corner," explains the architect. "A player should flirt with one of the fairway bunkers to get the best angle to the green."

The fourth, ninth and 12th are challenging par 3's, recalling Jones' work at Briar's Creek. Depending on the tee box chosen, either more or less of the hazard can be confronted from the tee, as the angle of attack changes. The ninth is a paramount example of this, requiring a 200-yard carry over the wetlands to reach

either the putting surface or the bailout area. Succeeding tee boxes diminish the distance and mitigate the angle to accommodate less-skilled players. Forward tees on the greenside of the hazard eliminate any forced carry of the wetland on this and all of the one-shot holes.

The esteemed designer draws a thoughtful analogy between his high-profile conceptions around town and that of his best-known predecessor in the region: "In the mid-20's, Seth Raynor did excellent work at the Country Club of Charleston and Yeamans Hall," explains Jones. "There are similarities between the courses, but many differences also, in part because of the difference in terrain. The same can be said for my work at Briar's Creek and here at Ralston Creek. The courses are diverse, in different locations with different topography. But there are similarities in terms of the style of design."

The esteemed designer draws a thoughtful analogy between his high-profile conceptions around town and that of his best-known predecessor in the region ...

Eventually, the same type of stately homes that complement Fazio's Beresford Creek course will be seen on Ralston Creek, though it will be several years before the housing on the newer golf course becomes much more than an incidental presence. Adjacent or parallel fairways throughout the opening nine limit the number of homesites on the course itself. With generous setbacks and the residences mostly on the periphery, as opposed to the interior of the course, the golf experience should supersede the real estate component.

"I think Ralston Creek has an old, neoclassic look," continues Jones. "We've opted for stylized bunkers that bring to mind the work of Alister MacKenzie and A.W. Tillinghast." The one-shot 15th is a perfect example of such. It's simple and elegant with a plateau green guarded by a dangerous bunker and framed by a panorama of marsh. It already looks a hundred years old.

The greens are relatively small and contoured, yielding birdie putts for those skillful enough to land an approach shot on the proper level. Less-accurate strikers will need to negotiate subtle rolls and valleys to maintain par. But the real variance is vertical. It's a nice blend of raised and flush-to-the-fairway putting surfaces. This varies the approach options, allowing for balls that must fly to the green and ones that can be run or bounced towards the flag. It's a thoughtful combination.

> *Jones concludes by offering a unique analogy to describe the opportunity he's been given at Daniel Island. "To me, this is a situation that's reminiscent of Pinehurst, in the sand hill region of North Carolina."*

Jones concludes by offering a unique analogy to describe the opportunity he's been given at Daniel Island. "To me, this is a situation that's reminiscent of Pinehurst, in the sand hill region of North Carolina. This is a new town, and the developers have done an outstanding job with the entire island. The residential development, commercial district, tennis facility and open spaces and parks have all been executed to a very high standard. The real estate sales have been very impressive, as residents of the area move to this island and retirees settle here from other places. Tom Fazio and I are very fortunate that we were asked to get involved at the nascent stage of what is destined to become one of the great recreational and living communities in the Southeast." And the recent Rees Jones contribution to the golf landscape has added another vital component to the burgeoning recreational options at one of Charleston's most intriguing new addresses.

Number 4, Par 3

*P*ros and crack amateurs have a nickname for the practice range. Actually, the nickname refers to the collection of balls at their feet, known as "the rock pile." Next time you're paired with a real player, when he cannons a drive down the center stripe or floats an approach shot right at the flag, profess your admiration. You might hear something like, "Well I hope I can hit a decent shot once in a while, the amount of time I spend on the rock pile."

Personally speaking, I'm no geologist.

Personally speaking, I'm no geologist. I'm also not one to embrace heavy lifting, at least if it can be avoided. But I like to hit golf balls as much as anybody else, just not on the range, at least not for more than five or ten minutes. And therein lies one of the unsung advantages of a Lowcountry summer. During that time of year, with kids out of school and folks on vacation, morning traffic thins just a bit on the highways, and late afternoon traffic is all but nonexistent on our fairways.

In the heat of a Charleston summer, most of the tee times are scheduled for morning, or early afternoon at the latest. Which means an enterprising golfer can arrive on the first tee somewhere between quitting time and the dinner hour, and get around the course with an expediency way beyond the ken of a typical weekend golfer. It's a magic number, akin to the four-minute mile or a .400 batting average. Eighteen holes in 90 minutes. Or two hours if you prefer a more leisurely pace, or searching for the occasional lost ball, or re-doing putts, chips and approaches that aren't to your liking.

The point is that solo golf, focused golf, golf-on-a-mission as twilight approaches, is an extraordinarily efficient way to play. It's not for everyone, because some folks are at least as concerned with winning a Nassau, or socializing with their buddies, or puttering around with their spouses. But for those who are content to confront the course and not a specific opponent, those who want to count strokes, try and shoot a certain number and get around in the fewest blows possible, it's a wonderful and cost-effective use of time.

One of golf's great appeals is the social aspect, and everyone who plays regularly enjoys the easy camaraderie of their regular group. The wide range of bets, presses and games-within-the-game is another attraction, and a huge percentage of casual golfers couldn't care less what they shoot, as long as they take five or ten bucks from their opponent.

But for those who are satisfied with the simple act of striking the ball, particularly on the playing field and not the practice range, solo flying through the summer months is a super alternative. It's not as if the courses are totally deserted. There are sporadic singles and twosomes about, but they're normally quick to wave you through. Rarely will you encounter any type of extended wait as the day turns dusky. Play a couple of compressed rounds, or even half-rounds, and the next time you're out with your pals, no matter how much fun the group might be, there'll be a little voice inside your head reminding you of all the other things you could be accomplishing in the same time frame.

There are sporadic singles and twosomes about, but they're normally quick to wave you through. Rarely will you encounter any type of extended wait as the day turns dusky.

I admire inveterate "rangers," those legions of serious golfers who can spend an hour rhythmically beating balls, working their way methodically through the golf bag, trying to hone a repeating and dependable swing. I myself reject the rock pile. But I respect your perseverance in the fading light, and salute you as I make the turn, barreling towards the tenth tee.

Cassique

KIAWAH ISLAND CLUB

Number 14, Par 4

To understand why Cassique is such an innovative course design, a bit of background is in order. "The original golf course here at the Kiawah Island Club is Tom Fazio's River Course," begins Head Professional Martin Shorter. "It's a beautifully classic Lowcountry layout, very traditional for this part of the world. But as the membership grew we needed an additional golf course. The concept that evolved was to do something totally different."

"The management team decided to hire Tom Watson as the course designer, though he hadn't worked on a solo design in the United States up until that point," continues Shorter, who was the original head pro when the course opened in 1999. He came back to the club in 2003 after a stint at Doonbeg in Ireland, a sister facility to the 36-hole Kiawah Island Club.

Watson is a five-time British Open champion and a huge fan of links golf. The design he submitted was totally unlike the existing Fazio layout, and eminently walker-friendly, which was another huge plus. "Cassique features a wonderful clubhouse that resembles an English manor home, which complements the course," explains the pro. "So the two golf layouts at the club offer a totally diverse experience for the membership."

So Cassique is unique, both in name and architectural style. Its odd mounding, occasional blind shots, "tribute holes," steeply terraced fairways and intermittent angularity might strike some traditionalists as strange. But many visitors, this correspondent included, find it to be one of the most delightful tests of the game in all of greater Charleston. It offers a tremendous diversity of holes, has some of the most stunning long-range views in the Lowcountry, is tough enough but player-friendly in the same breath. It is on the very short list, one of a handful of courses (minus the thumb and pinkie) of Charleston must-plays.

More than a million cubic feet of earth was displaced in turning this formerly flat tomato field into the memorably exhilarating golf adventure it's become. Critics might call some of the Irish and Scottish tributes Watson has implemented into the design derivative, but it's just another distinctive element of this avant-garde blueprint. The steeply banked approach fronting the green at the par-5 second hole lords over a "wee burn," modeled after the 16th at Turnberry. A less-than-solid effort to find the putting surface will find the closely mown bank and roll back into the narrow water hazard guarding the green.

More than a million cubic feet of earth was displaced in turning this formerly flat tomato field into the memorably exhilarating golf adventure it's become.

The par-5 sixth has "spectacle bunkers," in homage to Carnoustie, which will ensnare a poorly conceived second shot. The ninth green features a massive false front, a replica of Ireland's famed links at Ballybunion. Apparently this feature has been softened a bit since the course opened. But it's still such a dramatic landform one wonders if the modification involved the removal of a green-side escalator that shuttled players from the fairway up to the putting surface proper.

In a golf course chock-full of curiosities, the most notable feature is the myriad options available on holes four through six. It's a bit muddled in the telling, not to mention the playing, at least the first couple of times through. The short par-4 fourth hole has a single tee box, but two separate greens. When the green in use is elevated and to the right, the hole is called "pulpit." When the green is low left, the hole is known as "nip and tuck." If the day's routing is to the lower green, then the succeeding par-3 fifth hole is played uphill to the pulpit green, which is also the pinnacle of "Mt. Watson," the highest point on the

property. If the par 4 is played to the "pulpit" green, then the succeeding par-3 tee shot is downhill to a separate green used expressly for that purpose. The tee shot on the par-5 sixth is either at ground level or on the crest of Mt. Watson, depending on whether the par 3 is played up towards the "pulpit" green, or downhill to the extra green. It's as confusing to play as it is to describe, but the rationale is quite simple: The membership is afforded a different routing and the opportunity to hit varied golf shots midway through the opening nine, depending on the day. It's a welcome option that adds even more variety to a course that has a multitude to begin with.

Watson and design associate Charlie Arrington of Kiawah Development Partners played some wonderful visual tricks from the tee box. To modify an old slogan, what you see is not what you get. "It doesn't play as difficult as it looks," continues the head pro. "Standing on the tee box, a first-timer is thinking, 'Where am I supposed to hit it?' But the driving corridors are actually quite generous upon inspection. They have to be, because the wind can be such a factor." Nowhere are these words truer than on the second hole. A yanked tee ball looks to sail into a heather-filled oblivion but will actually come to rest on a wide swath of fairway indiscernible from the teeing grounds.

"The best way to cut down on three-putting," opined the renowned ball-striker, "is to hit it closer to the flagstick."

Greens are quite large, again to factor the wind. Undulations, knobs and shelves are the watchwords, and reaching in regulation is no guarantee of par. Those who continually find themselves on the wrong side of the green shouldn't lament their poor luck, but instead remember Ben Hogan's famous words of advice. "The best way to cut down on three-putting," opined the renowned ball-striker, "is to hit it closer to the flagstick."

Even the awesome concentration of Hogan would be tested by the magnificent 15th hole. This mesmerizing and challenging par 5 has few if any equals in the region. On a course filled with panoramic views, there are none finer than the sweeping expanse of Captain Sam's Inlet, stretching to the southeast. A big drive to the right-hand portion of this split fairway allows a solid striker to reach in two blows, although a drifting approach shot will find the weeds at the edge of the inlet. Well-placed bunkering necessitates a thoughtful lay-up shot for those who opt for the conservative route. While there are many worthy candidates for the honor of Cassique's finest hole, suffice it to say that the 15th will always be a finalist.

This is an outsized golf course by virtually any definition. The greens, the views, the bunkering and the imagination it took to conceive. It's the antithesis of the area standard, the low-lying, low-profile courses that populate greater Charleston. It's a busy course, with massive mounding, pot bunkers, burns and staircase fairways. It's almost as if Watson and company decided to insert too many features, too many visuals into the mix. But the course is decidedly more about fun than funhouse. It may not be traditional, but it's very special nonetheless. Early critics might've called it contrived, a bit too manufactured. But as the landscape has grown in, the edges softened by time and wind, those provocative charges have ceased to be relevant.

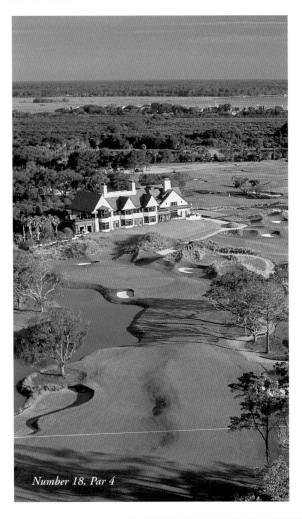

Number 18, Par 4

The definition of "Cassique" is leader, a respectful name given by Spanish explorers to coastal Indian chieftains. It's an apt name for this indelible golf experience. Truly a match made in heaven, as Cassique is one of the unquestioned leaders in the Charleston golf scene.

The definition of "Cassique" is leader, a respectful name given by Spanish explorers to coastal Indian chieftains.

One last thing about this world-beater: It's a massive piece of property, stretching acre upon untold acre through forest, marshland and all points in between. But the kick is that it's really a simple walking course, the commute between green and tee is negligible in almost every case. From the 17th tee, one can see Mt. Watson, the sixth fairway and the eighth green, all of which are well into the middle distance. As a player walks to the final tee and gazes left across an expansive marsh, they can view the putting surface on the par-3 13th, a superlative hole that was completed less than an hour before. From these vantage points, it's hard to believe one has managed to circumvent such a wide expanse of terrain in a few hours time, but that's part of the beauty, the magic of this incredible golf course. The game here is so enrapturing, the setting so all-consuming, it's easy to lose track of the time and the miles slipping by. Chalk it up to the mystique of Cassique.

*T*here are a number of people responsible for Kiawah Island's evolution as a major destination in the golf world. But knowledgeable observers would never argue this point: Nobody has been more important to the growth of its golf scene than Pat McKinney, the president of Kiawah Island Real Estate Company.

Nobody has been more important to the growth of its golf scene than Pat McKinney.

His early success on Hilton Head might've had much to do with mastering the soft sell. But when he first came to Kiawah, he changed the very fabric of management's attitude about golf because of his hard line.

McKinney began his career in the early 70's as a 21-year-old real estate salesman in Sea Pines, on the southern tip of Hilton Head. Working under Jim Chaffin and Jim Light, the wunderkind was named vice president of sales by 23. When the Kuwait Investment Company purchased Kiawah Island in 1974 for $17.4 million, they hired the Sea Pines Company to serve as the development's managing entity. "In 1975, I came up from Hilton Head to interview for the job as sales manager on Kiawah," recalls McKinney. "There was very little in the way of development at that time, just a single road cut and perhaps 20 beach cottages on that road."

McKinney was enamored with golf, which was one of the main reasons he enjoyed living on Hilton Head. He immediately saw Kiawah's potential as a development, but was dismayed at management's attitude towards golf, which he felt had inadvertently been relegated to secondary status. "It quickly became apparent our views on golf were different. They envisioned a 4,800-yard, executive-style course that could be played in three hours. It was adjacent to what was then the focal point of the development,

The Kiawah Inn. The thinking at that time was that conventioneers didn't have half a day to play golf, and this short course would fill their needs adequately." McKinney, only 25 at the time, disagreed vehemently, and wasn't shy about voicing his opinion. "I was probably a bit bolder than I should've been," he continues with a laugh. "But I was frank. I told them the island was beautiful, the property had huge potential. But I'd only be interested in the job on one of two conditions: Either drop the real estate prices by 25 percent, or find a way to make the golf course at least a par 70, so we could claim it was a regulation golf course."

The up-and-coming real estate mogul had a dual motivation. Sure, he loved the game dearly, unlike the mostly indifferent management team that was then assembled around him, and he wanted to stay close to it. But the larger reason has to do with the psychology of the sale process, which he understood intuitively very early in his career. "You don't buy island or vacation property on logic," he says flatly. "You buy on emotion. You buy based on your family, where you want to gather lifetime memories and create long-standing traditions. You don't sell it by the square foot, but instead by perception."

"You don't buy island or vacation property on logic," he says flatly. "You buy on emotion."

Having experienced the proprietary nature of his Hilton Head clients, people who took great pride in their renowned backyard courses like Harbour Town and the other Sea Pines offerings, McKinney knew that attempting to sell a compromised golf experience like what was being planned on the drafting table would be an uphill battle. "I listened to the arguments the planners used on me, trying to convince me that it wasn't just a par-3 course, and the integrity of the holes wouldn't be compromised and things of that nature. I knew our sales staff would have to make the same arguments over and over with potential buyers, corporate clients and the like. You'd have to mollify them about the golf experience before you could ever even attempt to discuss real estate." He convinced the brass that standing pat would be a crucial error, but standing by Pat would lead to big things. The rest, as they say, is history.

Visionary he may be, but he's no soothsayer. "I never would've envisioned seven championship courses sprouting on the property," he claims with a smile, referring to the current configuration of five resort and two private courses on or adjacent to the island.

He convinced the brass that standing pat would be a crucial error, but standing by Pat would lead to big things.

Tommy Cuthbert has been in lockstep with McKinney for decades. He's marveled at the continued growth and emergence of Kiawah Island in the golf world, growth that was precipitated in large part because McKinney saw how integral the sport would be to the resort's future. "Pat is just a quality individual," says Kiawah's original director of golf, who relinquished his post to Roger Warren in 2003. "We became acquainted when he interviewed me for the first head professional job at our very first golf course some 30 years ago. We've become really close friends over the years. He's respected throughout the community, has tremendous foresight, intelligence and is a very charitable man. Kiawah is fortunate to have a man of his capabilities running the real estate division."

Just like the field goal kicker who wins the Super Bowl in the waning seconds, or the jump shooter that scores the winning basket as time expires, McKinney's "line in the sand" could easily have been a career-defining moment. But a dozen years later, he made an even bolder move. After leaving Kiawah in the late 70's due to further differences with the foreign-management team, McKinney became a partner and vice president of sales and marketing at Wild Dunes on Isle of Palms. His tenure was highlighted by helping to facilitate the construction of the Links and Harbor courses, both designed by Tom Fazio.

But when the Kuwaitis were ready to divest themselves of what had become something of a white elephant in the late 80's, McKinney jumped at the chance to come back to Kiawah, this time as an ownership partner.

"My partner, Frank Brumley, and I put the property under a 90-day option in December of '87." Originally a math major at Emory before matriculating at Georgia State, McKinney wrote the 25-page financial pro forma himself. "I went back to crunch the numbers with what was then considered a portable, or at least a "luggable" PC. It was the size of a sewing machine, and I worked on that machine practically nonstop between Christmas and New Year's to make the numbers work." It took a couple of fits and starts, but they eventually sewed up the deal. Their $100 million offer didn't pass muster, but eventually McKinney and Brumley joined forces with the Darby, Way and Long families of Charleston, raised the ante to $105 million, and took control of the property in the summer of 1988. At the time, it was the largest real estate transaction in South Carolina's history.

Golf and real estate are all about the numbers, and McKinney's tally in both fields is awfully impressive. On the course, he credits an out-of-body experience that lead to a career-low 65 at Country Club of Charleston in 2001. "It's not that hard a course," is how he rationalizes it, though he's astute enough to know that shooting a 75, never mind a 65, is beyond the wildest dreams of most players no matter how toothless the track might be. "I never quite made it to a scratch handicap," he exclaims with a tinge of regret, likely one of few regrets this overachiever has ever known. "The lowest handicap index I ever had was about 1.5 or so." On the one hand, an 18-hole score like the one he rung up at the Country Club that fateful day offers bragging rights for a lifetime. But compared to some bigger McKinney numbers, it's strictly locker room or happy hour fodder.

"I never quite made it to a scratch handicap," he exclaims with a tinge of regret, likely one of few regrets this overachiever has ever known.

Consider this: Kiawah Resort Associates purchased Kiawah Island for the aforementioned $105 million in 1988. Since the purchase, they've had a total of

$2.5 billion in sales. Here are some fast facts in bite-sized form that make his accomplishments a bit more comprehensible. When McKinney first came on the scene in '76, the average lot price was about $20,000. Upon their purchase in '88, that average price was $120,000. By the end of 2003, the number was $620,000. Housing went from $90,000 to $620,000 to $1.2 million at the same benchmarks. You could imagine McKinney borrowing the line made famous by late baseball-great Roberto Clemente, and altering it for his own purpose: "Kiawah's been berry, berry good to me."

Family and faith are the twin touchstones of McKinney's life outside the office, in addition to that eccentric habit of whacking a tiny ball through a meadow. "Many of us grow up in households where religious faith is somewhat important," says McKinney, now in his mid 50's. "As we become young adults ourselves, busy with life and business pursuits, we tend to de-emphasize that aspect of life. When we get older and have children of our own, realizing we can have such a profound influence on their lives, some of us tend to return to the values our parents taught us. I know I certainly have," explains the deacon at First Scot's Presbyterian Church. "My faith has become an increasingly important part of my life."

Family and faith are the twin touchstones of McKinney's life outside the office, in addition to that eccentric habit of whacking a tiny ball through a meadow.

What has never increased, because it's been unwavering since the beginning, is McKinney's love of family. "Pam and I have been married since the mid-80's. I asked her to marry me on Valentine's Day, and she said, 'Before I answer that question let me ask one of my own. Do you have any plans to leave Charleston?' I said no, she said yes, and we've had a wonderful life together."

Kelley is the eldest daughter, a 20-something marketing professional with a master's degree from the University of South Carolina. Amy is the middle child, a thriving student at Furman University, where she's been joined by her younger sister, Sally.

Though he oversees a staff of 25 sales professionals, the once-and-future golf nut still takes to the

links about once or twice a week. He spends his fair share of time in the office, and part of his day commuting, of all things. This Kiawah real estate baron has chosen to live in downtown Charleston, though the family has enjoyed a variety of different vacation homes in close proximity to the office, mostly used in summers or for holidays. "With the kids in school and involved in civic and church-related activities, it's always made sense for us to be downtown."

McKinney has always found time to give back to the game he loves, the game that in many ways has defined the ultra-successful career he's enjoyed. He's a past president of the South Carolina Golf Association, and his input as a member of the USGA Mid-Amateur Championship Committee was instrumental in the 2009 Mid-Am being awarded to the Kiawah Island Club.

He was also the advisory general chairman of Kiawah's bellwether golf moment, the legendary 1991 Ryder Cup. "I couldn't stand the pressure of the final day," concludes McKinney, recalling the excruciating finish of the competition, which ultimately came down to the final putt. "I left the golf course, rushed back to my condo and watched the conclusion in peace and quiet."

An amazing bit of irony, upon reflection. He might have lost his nerve in the crucible of the Cup. But far more importantly, McKinney could handle the pressure of the island's purchase in 1988. And partly because of his intelligence, work ethic, salesmanship and vision, untold thousands of golfers, property owners and guests will enjoy peace and quiet on Kiawah for many years to come.

An amazing bit of irony, upon reflection. He might have lost his nerve in the crucible of the Cup.

The River Course

KIAWAH ISLAND CLUB

Number 17, Par 3

There was a grizzled golf curmudgeon holding court one afternoon in an airport lounge. He was claiming there was a homely Tom Fazio golf course somewhere in the upper Midwest, and that he'd been there and seen it himself. I didn't buy it for a moment. Like the Loch Ness Monster or Sasquatch, until I see it with my very own eyes, I can't believe it exists.

As a longtime observer and admirer of his work, I've developed a theory called Tom Fazio's Upward Mobility, or alternatively, his "Reverse Downward Spiral." Think of a typical downward spiral. A guy gets downsized and loses his job. This precipitates a chain reaction where one thing leads to another, all of them bad. Losing the job might mean losing the car. No transportation means no availability to work, and

eventually he loses his home, then his family, self-respect, etc., etc.

Now think of Fazio, but in the opposite light. He builds a world-class golf course, like the Links at Wild Dunes. Developers take note and offer him another beautiful piece of land, perhaps in the mountains of western North Carolina, to do it again. This new course, let's call it Wade Hampton, attracts more attention, and another developer unafraid to reach in his wallet, for argument's sake let's say Steve Wynn, gives him an unlimited budget. As legend has it, this unlimited budget is exceeded, and the end result is Shadow Creek in Las Vegas. This showpiece attracts the attention of even more developers, who continue to offer even finer parcels of land, and before you

Foreground, Number 17, Par 3. Backgrond, Number 18, Par 4

know it, you hold the unofficial title of America's Greatest Living Architect. Or as it was recently said in Golf Digest, "Fazio is the 800-pound gorilla of golf course architecture, a man who seemingly gets any project he wants, any place he wants, with any budget he wants."

The River Course at Kiawah Island, yet another bold hue in a seemingly limitless supply of colors in the architect's palette.

This brings us to the circumstances surrounding the creation of The River Course at Kiawah Island, yet another bold hue in a seemingly limitless supply of colors in the architect's palette. The course occupies some 300 whiz-bang acres of prime real estate on this ultra-expensive island. Fazio being Fazio, the developers made certain that the course dictated the land and not the other way around. Holes three, four and five cross to the east side of the main drag, known as the Kiawah Island Parkway. Apparently the architect said he could fit the entire course on the west side of the road, but would be able to produce a more memorable routing by using the adjunct parcel across the street. So the powers that be made it happen.

"The River Course is very distinctive, with a special character," begins the man who created it. "The reasons for this are many. There's a huge bass pond that parallels some of the front-side holes you see upon arrival. Then you look out over the marsh, and come into the view of a stately and strong clubhouse. The Kiawah River sets the tone for the golf course, and the 18 holes meander in all different directions. It was built after Hurricane Hugo came through, and the storm created open spaces on the property that didn't exist previously. By excavating the land for lakes and water hazards, we used the surplus dirt to create dunes, variety and elevation changes. The end result is a course that starts strongly and improves as it progresses. Players can't wait to get to the next tee, to see what comes next."

The starting holes at The River Course are a little game of "Can You Top This?" The opening par-4 dogleg is pretty, but the tee shot on the par-5 second, which must carry a yawning waste bunker peppered with love grasses, is gorgeous. The short third with a bunker-framed green and water right is even better. And so on. The short par-4 fifth is notable because of

dual greens. The green short left is tucked behind a lagoon, daring a big bopper to try and reach it from the tee. The other green is perched on a plateau to the right, perhaps 30 yards farther and more accessible from the tee.

Some of the mild criticism directed towards this 1995 effort, silly as it sounds, is that it is too beautiful. Some describe it as an arboretum, a flower garden or wildlife refuge first, a compelling golf experience second. Nonsense. Like many of his finest creations, the challenge and difficulty of Fazio's course is masked a bit by the comely surroundings, but the course, with its 142 slope and 74.7 rating, stretching to 7,000-plus yards, is no yawner by any means. (Littler sticks would do well at 6,600 or even 6,200 yards, sloped at 137 and 134, respectively.)

Some describe it as an arboretum, a flower garden or wildlife refuge.

That said, in all the tropical or semi-tropical climates this correspondent has chased a golf ball, never have there been so many encounters with such sizeable gators. Ten and 12 feet long by the look of things, though no one in the group dared pull out the tape measure. Not hard to understand, because the housing presence is so incidental, the few estates on the property so spread out and set back, this course has an element of wild missing from 95 percent of the facilities in the immediate area.

The scenery changes a bit down the homestretch. Holes 14 through 16 move away from the water features so prevalent earlier on. Here it's a bit of back and forth, a pair of strong par 4's and a par 5, delineated by wide swaths of love grass-infused waste areas. The penultimate hole is a beautiful long-view par 3, and the finisher is as intimidating as anything that came before. It's a daunting par-4 dogleg, a forced carry off the tee, with golden marshland bracketing the left side of the fairway. It's a fitting conclusion to a world-class course.

The professional staff comments that the wax myrtles, sweet grasses, river views, bass pond, multiple lagoons, abundant wildlife and other natural features make a round a sensory experience that few other courses can match. First-time players tend to get caught up in the beauty of the surroundings, and sometimes sublimate the golf experience because of it. In many cases, it takes several rounds before the strategic challenge of the course asserts itself fully, and the golfer is able to devote his entire concentration to the task at hand. The course is more than window dressing, as evidenced by the commitment of the USGA to bring the 2009 Mid-Amateur Championship to The River Course and its sister facility, Cassique.

The professional staff comments that the wax myrtles, sweet grasses, river views, bass pond, multiple lagoons, abundant wildlife and other natural features make a round a sensory experience that few other courses can match.

In the appendix of Fazio's colorful and informative book "Golf Course Designs," there are exactly 125 courses listed. You might think the author/architect would need a minute or so to collect his thoughts on The River Course, considering it's only 18 of approximately 2,250 golf holes he's created. But he takes less than five seconds to start describing the ebb and flow of play.

"The first five holes are open, and the sixth is a downhill par 3 over a marsh with mully grass and long-range views, and it gets better. Then you play adjacent to Bass Pond as the front nine concludes and the character changes again. The back nine begins with tight, tree-lined holes, and then a canal influences both the tee shot and second on a par 5. After that, the course widens into open spaces midway through the back nine, and then the last two holes offer a different character altogether, including a very tough finisher."

You can't ask Fazio to choose the favorite of his six children, and an equally uncomfortable task is choosing his favorite hole on The River Course.

You can't ask Fazio to choose the favorite of his six children, and an equally uncomfortable task is choosing his favorite hole on The River Course. "Fourteen through 16 are among the best on the back, and they're not even marsh holes. You can't ignore the sixth hole, you have to mention the par-5 eighth which skirts the pond, and the ninth might be the best of them all," he concludes with a shrug. So many holes, so little time, as the saying goes. "It's that good. I believe that emphatically." After close inspection, Mr. Fazio, so do we.

I distinctly remember the first time I hit a golf shot and thought to myself, "I've got it."

"It," of course, is the secret of the game, the ability to consistently and confidently hit smooth, powerful shots in the direction intended. This epiphany, a false one, as you can well imagine, occurred well over a dozen years ago up in my home state of Massachusetts. I was a young buck just past 30, had recently broken 80 for the first time, and uttered those three fateful words to myself just a couple of months later. The nitty-gritty specifics are lost to memory, of course, but the general recollection goes like this:

I was within a few shots of par on the elevated 16th tee, a 420-yard dogleg-left with plenty of tree and mounding trouble both left and right.

I was within a few shots of par on the elevated 16th tee, a 420-yard dogleg-left with plenty of tree and mounding trouble both left and right. The drive wasn't an award winner, but was more than serviceable. It was down the center with decent length, and I realized that even by bogeying into the clubhouse from there the scorecard tally would remain under 80. Full of brio and insouciance, the fateful statement lodged in my head. Unfortunately, the next golf shot lodged in a bush left of the fairway after an ungodly pull, and after hacking my way to a triple bogey or more (who can remember?) I limped home with an 81 or 82.

Many other times in the succeeding decade those same three words floated through my cerebral cortex. How couldn't they really, after shooting four consecutive rounds in the 70's, or carding back-to-back 75's, things of that nature. But of course you never really get golf. Golf just gets you.

These remembrances of youthful naiveté came rushing back just recently, as I completed the first round of the New Year. I hadn't had a club in hand in some three weeks, and a busy schedule had limited links time to just a couple of rounds since Thanksgiving. The abysmal beginning to the round came as no surprise, as I was already double digits over par only a third of the way through. But suddenly the ball began drawing, both off the tee and towards the flag, evaporated distance suddenly reappeared, an all-too-rare eagle putt was attempted, and the last dozen holes were covered within a few shots of par.

However, after literally dozens and dozens of past experiences where I thought "it" was suddenly understood, this time there was no such illusion. The last few years have been good in many ways, but not necessarily on the fairways. You know how a dog that has been beaten too often is sketchy and a bit gun-shy? That's the unfortunate metamorphosis I've undergone myself on the links, hoping for the best but generally expecting the worst.

Now when things start to hum, pars come easily and a birdie putt is a distinct possibility on almost every hole; there are no proclamations, internal or external, about "it." Instead, I just enjoy the ride, enjoy the run, enjoy the "click" of a ball struck somewhere near the center of the clubface and do the best I can for as long as it lasts. Because there are no more illusions harbored about "getting it" anymore. Too many variables, too many moving parts, too many different swing thoughts, theories and bad habits are part of my personal milieu.

Until the ghost of Hogan or Jones visits me in the wee hours and I can transmogrify into the scratch or near-scratch player I once had dreamed of being, I'll just take whatever I get ...

Until the ghost of Hogan or Jones visits me in the wee hours and I can transmogrify into the scratch or near-scratch player I once had dreamed of being, I'll just take whatever I get, and hope there's more bad than good. It was said succinctly 350 words ago, but bears repeating here at essay's end. Like most everyone else who's ever taken stick in hand, false hopes have become harsh reality. Nobody (except Tiger, Jack, Byron, etc.) ever "gets" golf. Golf just gets you.

Snee Farm

They began appearing on the scene in the early to mid-50's, and 15 or so years later, somewhere around Woodstock and the moonwalk (Neil Armstrong's, not Michael Jackson's) the golf cart was firmly imbedded in the fabric of our nation's golf scene.

Veteran architect George Cobb came to Mount Pleasant and routed Snee Farm Country Club just a couple of years later, in the early 70's. But the man who pioneered much of the early golf on Hilton Head thankfully maintained his walking sensibility. Because of all the courses in and around greater Charleston, there are few more conducive to walking then Snee Farm.

With the exception of a couple of truly old-guard clubs looking forward to centennial celebrations in a few decades time, most of greater Charleston's private clubs are a bit more of the Johnny-come-lately variety. Not so at Snee, where kids who might've dabbled with golf and enjoyed the flourishing tennis and swimming programs decades earlier have rejoined as adult members. Having grown up with fond memories of the club and its amenities, they're now exposing their children to the same childhood pleasures. "Not just a country club, but a way of life," is a marketing slogan rooted in fact.

Snee Farm also generates fond memories for thousands of choice amateurs, skilled golfers whose visits may have been brief, but vivid nonetheless.

The renowned Rice Planters Invitational Tournament is just a couple of years younger than the golf course. The venue and the elite amateur event are virtually indistinguishable from each other, so long have they been associated. The Rice Planters, considered to be among the top-seven annual amateur events in the nation, has been a fixture at the club for more than 30 years.

The Rice Planters, considered to be among the top-seven annual amateur events in the nation, has been a fixture at the club for more than 30 years.

Dick Horne is a well-known area golf figure. He's a founding member of the club, the founder and driving force behind the Rice Planters event and a multiple club champion and senior champion. "When the tournament began in 1973, we had mostly local fields for a few years," explains Horne, now in his late 60's. "Our first high-profile champion was Andy Bean, who won the event in 1975," he says, referring to the native Georgian who made the Rice Planters his last amateur event before embarking on a professional career that included 11 PGA Tour victories.

Water is at least an incidental presence on 17 holes at Snee Farm. Only on the short par-3 fourth is a player guaranteed to leave the ball retriever holstered. Many of the remaining holes have water on the periphery, with others featuring hazards front and center. Of course the word "incidental," as used in the opening sentence of this paragraph, is a relative thing. A respected instructor, who unlike many of today's more-renowned "golf professors" tests his game regularly in tournament play, once said memorably, "No matter how well the round may be going, you're always just one swing from disaster." On that same topic, the water is only incidental if you manage to avoid it.

Water is at least an incidental presence on 17 holes at Snee Farm.

The professional staff indicates that the course plays tougher than it looks, which is due in large part to the petite and well-bunkered greens, some-

thing of a George Cobb trademark. Snee Farm might be considered a second- or even third-shot golf course, but once again everything is relative. While a typical neighborhood retiree might need three blows at minimum to find the putting surface on the 610-yard sixth hole, an average Rice Planters invitee will cannon a drive over the corner of this dogleg-right and have a long iron or fairway wood into the green. Eagles are rare because the green isn't particularly receptive to such a long shot in, but chip-and-putt birdies are just as common as pars. Speaking of easy birdies, the much shorter par-5 second hole truly plays as a par 4 for the college studs descending every summer, and offers one of the best birdie bids for the membership at large. It's only about 485 yards total, though there's water skulking about the landing zones. If the drive carries far enough down the fairway to have a look at the green, then knocking it on or at least near in two is a distinct possibility.

Tripp Cobb is a relatively new member of Snee Farm, and is distinguished not only by his youth but by his legacy.

The quartet of one-shot holes offer subtle distinctions a first-timer might not notice. Besides the aforementioned absence of water on the fourth, the hole is visually deceiving. It looks perfectly level but actually plays uphill. By contrast, the seventh looks uphill but truly plays to a slightly lower elevation. The 11th is considered the signature hole at Snee Farm, an expansive par 3 with long views and a water carry. The penultimate hole is in certain ways the most distinctive, not just of the par 3's but of all the holes on the golf course. No. 17 has two distinct sets of tees on either side of a small lagoon, separated by a narrow wooden bridge. One day the tee shot might be more than 220 yards, the next closer to 180. But beyond the length variance, the dual teeing grounds offer two different angles towards the sloped putting surface.

Tripp Cobb is a relatively new member of Snee Farm, and is distinguished not only by his youth but by his legacy. Officially known as George Cobb III, he really enjoys the fact that his home course is one of his granddad's creations, which has been the case through most of his life. "I grew up in West

Number 10 green from Number 11 tee

Virginia and my family is from Greenville. In both cases, we played most of our golf at one of my grandfather's courses," explains 30-something Tripp with understandable pride. "I think that Snee Farm is a wonderful place to play. It can be quite challenging because of the tributary of the nearby Wando River that runs throughout the course. But it's also lots of fun."

Like his grandfather did before him, Tripp makes his living in the golf business. His duties as a golf course irrigation salesperson keep him on the road throughout the Carolinas much of the time, and consequently he gets out to Snee Farm only a couple of times a month. This is in direct contrast to a large percentage of the membership, those regulars making their way round the premises with nearly the same frequency as the postman does the neighborhood. It's a testament to the playability of the layout that the course maintains its appeal and enjoyment despite such intimate familiarity. Of course, yet again, all is relative. Cobb III, with his couple of

rounds a month, is something of an old hand compared to the collegiate hotshots who descend upon Snee for the Rice Planters every summer.

" We've been very fortunate to have had some high-profile champions," says Dick Horne, who almost won his own event in its sophomore year ...

"We've been very fortunate to have had some high-profile champions," says Dick Horne, who almost won his own event in its sophomore year, losing a sudden-death playoff to close friend Bill Harvey. In the late 70's, Scott Hoch edged out Hal Sutton in a playoff, then Sutton returned the following year to win a title of his own. Former British Open champ and 2006 Ryder Cup captain Tom Lehman won the event in the early 80's, and the very next year Brandel Chamblee birdied the last two holes to edge out Scott Verplank by a shot.

Number 10, Par 4

Duffy Waldorf, Franklin Langham and Stewart Cink are all past champions, as is longtime ace amateur and current Champions Tour standout Allen Doyle, the only man to win the Rice Planters three separate times. But a short list of non-winners is even more impressive than the roster of champions. Eventual Major champions like Davis Love III, Jeff Sluman and Steve Jones tried their luck but couldn't capture top honors. Over time, the Rice Planters has grown from a local event to a national and now international event. In part because of its sterling reputation and legacy, in recent years the tournament has begun to attract top amateur players from Australia, New Zealand and other far-off points on the compass.

Eventual Major champions like Davis Love III, Jeff Sluman and Steve Jones tried their luck but couldn't capture top honors.

George Cobb passed away some 20 years ago, when Tripp was barely a teenager. But Tripp knew his architect grandfather well, and was fortunate to have spent time with him both on and off the golf course. "Most of his work was done before golf architecture went really high tech," concludes Tripp. "I admire that he could go off in the woods or on a coastal plain with nothing more than a topographic map and a compass and carve out golf holes that people still enjoy to this very day, some 40 years later." And George Cobb carved some of these very good holes north of Charleston at friendly, unpretentious Snee Farm.

Yeamans Hall

Number 10, Par 4

Pine Valley, generally regarded as the world's finest golf course, is tucked behind a down-at-the-heels amusement park off a busy thoroughfare in southern New Jersey. Augusta National, as anyone lucky enough to have attended the Masters knows, is separated from the strip mall sensibility of Washington Road, with its pancake houses, gas stations and convenience stores, by a privet hedge. And when approached from the direction of Charleston itself, those fortunate souls heading to Yeamans Hall in the nearby town of Hanahan pass through a utilitarian industrial park before turning off the through road and turning back the clock concurrently.

These three examples show more than that landscapes both frowzy and golf-phenomenal can exist contiguously. It also proves the inverse of a popular New Age expression, "The journey is more important than the destination." In each of these cases, it's the final destination that's essential, and not the journey to arrive there.

As golf courses are literally living, breathing organisms, they are in a constant state of flux. But the ongoing, orderly changes being imposed on Yeamans Hall are among the most dramatic and positive developments in all of Charleston. In the last decade, the raison d'etre of the course, the magnificent greens, have been brought almost all the way back to the design sensibilities of architect Seth Raynor. Thanks to the work of renowned architect Tom Doak and his dedicated crew, the course is drastically improved from what it was, and the golf world has taken notice. Though it's now more than 80 years old and had never been listed previously, Yeamans Hall made its initial appearance on *Golf Magazine's* list of the world's top-100 courses just recently.

"It's a very special place, hard to explain," says Director of Golf Claude Brusse. "It's a great golf course, you can play it every day and never tire of it. It's the greens that make it unique. Tom Doak and his crew came in here and did a great job."

Doak got the job restoring the Yeamans greens for speaking his mind. While he was still learning the ropes, before he became a high-profile "name" architect with courses like Pacific Dunes and Cape Kidnappers on his resume, Doak was best known as an architectural critic and pundit. In his well-received 1996 book, "The Confidential Guide to Golf Courses," he said in part: "...sad neglect has ravaged Yeamans Hall. Forty years of topdressing has rendered the existing greens as uninteresting, slightly raised mounds inside the shells of their former selves. Too bad about the greens, because fixed up, the course would be terrific." The greens committee chairman at the time understood the sensibility, and with good word of mouth coming from Camargo Club in Cincinnati, another Raynor treasure where Doak had received high marks for some sensitive restoration work, he was hired in Charleston. "He did the 13th green first, almost as a test," recalls Brusse, who, himself, got down and dirty working in the sod during the restoration process. "It turned out great, so we gave the whole contract to him."

Jim Urbina is Tom Doak's senior design associate, and has worked with the architect for some 15 years. He was knee deep at Yeamans Hall for the duration of the greens-renovation project, which began shortly before the millennium.

"A typical Seth Raynor green should be square and large," explains Urbina. "But changing mowing patterns and years of topdressing had altered the greens drastically. Imagine an upside-down coffee saucer in the middle of a green. That's what we were dealing with upon arrival. It was highly unusual, to say the least. The greens had shrunk to half their original size, and instead of being big and square they were little and rounded. Someone asked me what those greens looked like before we

started. All I could think to show as an example was a dinner plate which would embody the green, then turning it upside down on a big square placemat to represent how the old greens looked. Decade upon decade of topdressing will do that."

"I've seen many redan holes over the years, and the sixth at Yeamans is a great one," continues Urbina. "But it was particularly unsightly, with this round protuberance in the center of the green."

George Bahto is among the nation's leading experts on architect Seth Raynor. "Now that the greens have been restored to their original specifications, the next order of business is the bunkering," opines the author of "The Evangelist of Golf," a biography of Raynor's mentor Charles Blair Macdonald. "The course was originally a minefield of creative bunkering. But the membership had allowed 70-odd bunkers to grass-in over time, because, in my opinion, they thought the course played too difficult with all of them in place. When that bunker work is done, Yeamans Hall will be one of the top-five courses in the South. The ambience is just matchless. It's an unbelievable experience, like going back in time. Out there at the end of the marsh, the course is an entity unto itself."

According to Urbina, some of the lost bunkers are the result of encroaching tree growth and vegetation. The bunkers were outside the tree line and allowed to grow over. But longtime-superintendent Jim Yonce has been diligent about thinning the tree cover and battling the vegetation, thereby recovering bunkers that will eventually become part of the strategy once again.

There can be little argument that the two most significant and renowned courses in greater Charleston are Yeamans Hall and the Ocean Course on Kiawah Island. But the irony is that they are polar opposites in so many ways.

There can be little argument that the two most significant and renowned courses in greater Charleston are Yeamans Hall and the Ocean Course on Kiawah Island. But the irony is that they are polar opposites in so many ways. It goes beyond the contradictions of classic versus modern, parkland versus surfside, natural versus manufactured and extremely private versus world famous. The fact is that only a highly skilled player will make it around the Ocean Course with the same ball, unless the day is unusually calm. But as a wiseacre once memorably said, "You bring shame onto your family if you lose more than a sleeve of balls at Yeamans the entire season!"

That exaggeration underscores the point that this parkland beauty is quite generous off the tee, with almost a complete absence of water hazards. Fairway bunkering can cause some consternation, but the challenge of Yeamans Hall is on and around the marvelous green complexes, now thankfully restored to their original sensibilities.

Claude Brusse explains that the greens practically doubled in size post-renovation, going from a total square footage of 80,000 to almost 145,000. "Now we have two and even three greens within the green," continues the pro, who first came to Yeamans in 1993. "You can hit it anywhere on the fairway or beyond, and will usually be okay. The tricky part is hitting the approach shot to the proper portion of the green. Miss on the wrong side and getting it up and down is nearly impossible."

Simply put, some of the features that Doak rebuilt into the greens are eccentric but wonderful. Some call it a thumbprint, others a bathtub. The more common expression is a horseshoe, and this three-sided depression, seen on the short par-3 third hole and dramatic par-4 10th make hitting the proper quadrant of the green an imperative. Some greens have spines that divide the putting surfaces into left and right. There are false fronts, myriad opportunities to run the ball onto the surface, the aforementioned redan and an equally fine punchbowl. There's a little bit of everything going on green-wise.

"It's one of Raynor's best courses in terms of balance..."

"It's one of Raynor's best courses in terms of balance," continues Bahto. "The collection of classic holes made famous by Charles Blair Macdonald and Seth Raynor: the Biarritz, the Cape, the Short, the Redan, the Double Plateau, are really good. Taken as a whole, they make up one of his best overall efforts. If and when the bunkers are reinstated, it'll be fantastic. It was one of his greatest efforts to begin with, and if restored properly in the years to come, will be once again."

There's a sense of spaciousness at Yeamans Hall

Number 3, Par 3

which is a rarity in the modern golf world, and the reason is simple. It was originally conceived as a 36-hole facility, so the footprint of the golf course covers twice the land of a standard course. It's not just quantity, but quality as well. Yeamans Hall is located on a superior piece of land. The course is built on a natural sand ridge, which explains the property's exceptional drainage. This is no trifling matter in an area where soaking rains are common. There's also the naturally rolling topography, a definite rarity in the area.

There's a sense of spaciousness at Yeamans Hall which is a rarity in the modern golf world.

"We have instances of 30 to 40 feet of elevation change," continues Brusse, who estimates that 85 percent to 90 percent of the planned renovation work is done. "Unless you're using a bulldozer, that's a highly unusual situation around here."

While the vagaries of playing conditions and strategies employed have changed over the decades, along with membership philosophies and superintendents' attentions, the timeless appeal of Yeamans Hall endures for the golf classicist. "It's a place where the game goes back to its roots, where it's played for its own sake," says Jim Urbina. "At Yeamans, golf is the main thing. It's not something that's fit in between appointments and engagements. It's the central component of the club, and not just another diversion."

"At Yeamans, golf is the main thing. It's not something that's fit in between appointments and engagements. It's the central component of the club, and not just another diversion."
-- Jim Urbina

To restore the course thoroughly will require more work over time. "Although we've accomplished a lot, there's still much to be done," concludes Urbina. "The course currently plays much narrower than originally conceived by the architect. As the playing corridors widen once again, the strategy allowing for different lines of attack will surface once more. Raynor wanted the player to choose to approach the green from either the left or right side of the fairway. That option was lost as the fairways narrowed, but is being recovered as the course regains its original spaciousness. Bunkers that disappeared because they didn't seem to make sense will make sense once again when the course regains its original attributes. It's still a work in progress."

Pragmatically speaking, the architect calls Yeamans Hall a work in progress. But golfers, unaware of the ongoing transformation of Charleston's most renowned classic venue, will surely call it a work of art.

My late father was not only my first and favorite golf companion, but also a truly exceptional man. Karl Zuckerman was born in a peasant village near the Russia-Poland border in 1907, and suffered a childhood of want and deprivation more profound then most Americans of my generation could probably imagine. When he was very young, his father immigrated to the United States, but couldn't arrange for the rest of the family to follow. Soon afterward his mother contracted tuberculosis, dying in his arms at the outset of the First World War. My dad became the man of the house, and in charge of the welfare of his three younger sisters. He was 9 years old.

> *My dad became the man of the house, and in charge of the welfare of his three younger sisters. He was 9 years old.*

The siblings were separated, and shuttled between the homes of various neighbors and relatives. Compassion was at a premium. These reluctant hosts were indigent themselves, with neither the resources nor the inclination to treat these orphans with anything more than the very basics of human kindness. It was during this bleak period that my father was bayoneted in the leg by a Russian soldier while attempting to steal a few potatoes. The scar he carried on his leg from that day forward was an indelible reminder of the hunger of his youth.

After seven tortuous years, my father and his two surviving sisters finally made their way to America in 1921. Although his formal education had been interrupted when he was just a small boy, he quickly made up for lost time. He covered a decade's worth of schoolwork in a couple of years, and enrolled in The City College of New York. Initially, he had hopes of becoming a doctor, but instead turned his attention to the world of commerce. Although his family and associates thought him foolhardy, he opened up a millinery manufacturing operation in 1929, at the height of the Depression. He was more than smart and hardworking. He brought the same survival instinct to the business world that he had honed over all of those bitter Russian winters. He became successful, opened additional plants, and ended up employing virtually all of his relations.

When I was born in the waning years of the Baby Boom generation, my father was well past 50. By then he was an important man - a business success, a philanthropist, and a pillar in the community. I had a normal childhood, though ours was an unusual family. My dad was often mistaken for my grandfather. My half-brother, 30 years my senior, was old enough to be my dad, and my nephews were my contemporaries.

As a sports-crazy kid, I spent many hours playing catch with my father in the backyard, but to an outside observer it must have appeared peculiar. In matters of sport, he had the European soccer sensibility. He preferred to use his feet instead of his hands, and never once donned a baseball glove. Instead, he would field my throws to him on a short hop, stopping the ball with the sole of his shoe. It may not have looked like "Field of Dreams," but it seemed perfectly natural.

As a sports-crazy kid, I spent many hours playing catch with my father in the backyard, but to an outside observer it must have appeared peculiar.

He came to golf too late in life to achieve any real success, but it mattered little that his enthusiasm outstripped his abilities. He loved the game, and attempted to indoctrinate me to its subtle nuances as a preteen. There was a brief dalliance or two, but ultimately I resisted with the same vigor that enveloped virtually all of my contemporaries. Remember, this was several years before Tiger Woods was even born, and golf was decades away from being cool.

He came to golf too late in life to achieve any real success

Things changed when I got to high school. My dad was now in his late 60's, and he began to falter. After his first heart attack he recovered but was never quite the same. The illness took some of his spirit, the special spark that made him such a vital and engaging man. The problem was that as I got older, my dad got really old. When I was in college, he suffered another heart attack. Eventually he developed Alzheimer's disease. He put my mother through that special hell that only a primary caregiver knows, and had to be put in a nursing home. He died in 1991, and by then it was a blessing. He was prone to rage, uncomprehending, and indecipherable. One of my greatest sorrows was that he never really knew or could appreciate our firstborn daughter Karlian, his then two-year-old namesake, who would've brought light and life into an otherwise grievous existence.

During my youth and adolescence, my father taught me many lessons. He continually stressed to me the importance of charity, the value of reading, and the love of language. Although English wasn't his native tongue and he never lost his accent, he developed into a wonderful communicator himself; he was an inveterate reader and a thoughtful writer.

Another lesson he taught me was subliminal. Watching him age and deteriorate, I decided to stay young for my own children's sake. I didn't know it at the time, but the thought crosses my mind regularly now. My girls were born when I was just shy of and just past 30, and I revel in being able to keep up with them. Whether we're skiing, hiking or biking, I'm conscious of my relative youth, and I'm hopeful to be here for them and their children for many years to come.

I admired and loved my father; I couldn't have asked for better. Among the many gifts he bestowed was the golf seed he planted, a seed that lay dormant for close to 20 years. My boyhood indifference gave way to a latent fascination. If he could see how, through happenstance and a happy accident of fate, I've managed to combine his dual interests in golf and writing, I'm sure he'd be quite pleased.

In a small way, my father was a great man - wise, patient, compassionate and charitable. He survived until I was 30, but he lost much of his life force long before that. The inevitabilities of age took him from us much too soon, and that's a fact I'll regret for the rest of my life.

I admired and loved my father; I couldn't have asked for better. Among the many gifts he bestowed was the golf seed he planted, a seed that lay dormant for close to 20 years.

Charleston
WHERE TO STAY, WHOM TO ASK, WHERE TO PLAY

WHERE TO STAY

Because Charleston is such a tourist Mecca, there are untold hundreds of varying lodging options to suit every taste and budget. Here are two of the very best hotels in the region, one in the city and one by the sea.

The Sanctuary
843-768-6000 • 877-683-1234

Charleston Place
843-722-4900 • 800-611-5545

WHOM TO ASK

Here is a trio of reputable tour operators that can assist in planning a comprehensive golf-themed visit.

Charleston Golf Inc.
800-774-4444 • www.charlestongolfguide.com

Beach Walker Rentals
800-334-6308 • www.beachwalker.com

Southern Golf Tours Inc.
866-800-7002 • www.southerngolftours.net

WHERE TO PLAY

Within less than a hour's drive from the heart of the historic district, here are 21 venues golfers can choose from.

Charleston National Country Club
1360 National Drive • Mt. Pleasant, SC 29466
843-884-7799

City of Charleston Golf Course
2110 Maybank Highway • Charleston, SC 29412
843-795-6517

Coosaw Creek Country Club
4210 Club Course Drive • North Charleston, SC 29420
843-767-9000

Crowfield Plantation Golf & CC
300 Hamlet Circle • Goose Creek, SC 29445
843-764-4618

Dunes West Golf Club
3535 Wando Plantation • Mt. Pleasant, SC 29464
843-856-9000 • 888-955-1234

Golf Club at Wescott Plantation
5000 Wescott Club Drive • North Charleston, SC 29485
843-871-4424 • 866-211-4653

Kiawah Island Golf Resort
12 Kiawah Beach Drive • Kiawah Island, SC 29455
843-266-4050 • 800-654-2942

Cougar Point Golf Club
12 Kiawah Beach Drive • Kiawah Island, SC 29455
843-266-4020

Oak Point Golf Club
4394 Hope Plantation Drive • Johns Island, SC 29455
843-266-4100

The Ocean Course
12 Kiawah Beach Drive • Kiawah Island, SC 29455
Phone: 843-266-4670

Osprey Point Golf Club
12 Kiawah Beach Drive • Kiawah Island, SC 29455
843-266-4640

Turtle Point Golf Club
12 Kiawah Beach Drive • Kiawah Island, SC 29455
843-266-4050

Legend Oaks Plantation
118 Legend Oaks Way • Summerville, SC 29485
843-832-9816 • 888-821-4077

Links at Stono Ferry
4812 Stono Links Drive • Hollywood, SC 29449
843-763-1817

Patriots Point Links
1 Patriots Point Road • Mt. Pleasant, SC 29464
843-881-0042 • 877-709-5053

Pine Forest Country Club
1000 Congressional Boulevard • Summerville, SC 29483
843-851-1193

RiverTowne Country Club
1700 RiverTowne CC Drive • Mt. Pleasant, SC 29466
843-216-3777 • 866-216-3777

Seabrook Island Resort
3772 Seabrook Island Road • Johns Island, SC 29455
843-768-2529

Shadowmoss Plantation Golf Club
20 Dunvegan Drive • Charleston, SC 29414
843-556-8251 • 800-338-4971

Wild Dunes Harbor Course
5757 Palm Boulevard • Isle of Palms, SC 29451
843-886-2301 • 888-349-7921

Wild Dunes Links Course
5757 Palm Boulevard • Isle of Palms, SC 29451
843-886-2180 • 888-349-7921